BRINGING BACK THE BEAR

BRINGING BACK THE BEAR

HOW A COMMUNITY RESCUED BEAR RIVER MIGRATORY BIRD REFUGE

AL TROUT

Charleston, SC
www.PalmettoPublishing.com

BRINGING BACK THE BEAR

Copyright © 2021 by Al Trout

All rights reserved.

First Edition

Paperback ISBN: 978-1-68515-327-4

Table of Contents

ACKNOWLEDGMENTS

The restoration of Bear River Migratory Bird Refuge was a group effort, so was this manuscript. When composing my thoughts on paper, it is most difficult for me to set aside a quiet time to sit down, become physically still, and put my mind to the task. It took the encouragement of my wife Kathy to keep me on track to finish this manuscript. I cannot express my gratitude for her encouragement and companionship over the 51 years we have been married. Without her unconditional love and devotion, my career and involvement with the Refuge would not have been possible. Being with her is my daily place of refuge. The Lord gave us an additional sense of purpose over the years when we were blessed with three children – Chad, Ryan and Amy. In due time, their spouses Kelly, Ryan and Vanessa joined our family. Then best of all, we were blessed with five grandchildren who are now a daily source of joy and hope in this world that seems full of turmoil. Through the coming decades, I trust their lives will be enriched by vibrant landscapes and wildlife. May Bear River Refuge play a part in that experience.

This manuscript would not have been possible without the diligent editing of Anna Marie Singleton and her suggestions for improvement. She hung with me even thought I violated every rule of

English composition. She had a special way of simultaneously correcting my work and encouraging me to keep going.

Jon Bunderson, past president of the Friends of Bear River Refuge, has been a long term personal friend and source of encouragement. He was my link to the community of Brigham City.

To all my fellow employees, we shared the common goal of restoring the Refuge. Although I carried the authority of supervisor, the staff never worked "for me". Instead, they worked "with me."

My thanks to Karen Hogan, Alane Ferney and Palmetto Publishing for the cover design.

Finally, my good friend Lee Shirley said "you have got to write-up the restoration story." I felt pressured to say yes, then Lee died unexpectedly. That sealed the deal, I couldn't back out after that. But that's ok, I always felt the restoration was God's work anyway.

PROLOGUE

Originating high in the Uintah mountains, the Bear River winds its way through Wyoming, Idaho and Utah before terminating on the northern shores of the Great Salt Lake. After carving a meandering channel of 500 miles through mountains and valleys, it terminates by spreading into a myriad of small channels across a large shallow wetland complex. Unrivaled in size across the intermountain west, this delta is a premier habitat for wildlife.

For untold centuries the Bear River Delta sustained vast marshes, stretching across more than 400 hundred square miles, filling the landscape to the horizon and beyond. Fed by the terminal waters of the Bear River, these scenic wetlands flooded a portion of Great Salt Lake Basin with a slope so flat it dropped only one foot per mile. Adding to the scenic beauty, mountain ranges framed the east and west horizons. Bulrush, growing in erratic patchwork stands, graced the glassy clear waters with infinite patterns, creating an Eden-like scene with majestic mountain peaks framing both sunrises and sunsets. Unseen below the shallow water's surface, submerged aquatic plants filled the water column, providing a bountiful food source of seeds, stems and tubers. When adding a bountiful supply of protein from an abundance of midges and other insects, the area was a cornucopia of food, shelter, and nesting cover for millions upon millions of migratory birds. It was truly an Eden, a perfect garden for birds.

For eons, each day began with the gentle glow of butter-colored rays backlighting the jagged skyline of the Wasatch mountains. Minutes later, it drenched the wetlands in the valley far below in the soft, golden light of sunrise. Then, at day's end, a spectacular alpenglow blanketed the valley as the setting sun slipped behind the jagged horizon of the Promontory Mountain Range. Like the finale to a fireworks show, the sunset was concluded by horizontal beams of last-light flickering eastward from behind the spine of the Promontories and projecting on the west face of the parallel Wasatch Range. The light show would ignite reddish, golden hues until slowly extinguished by darkness. Seemingly attracted by the profound beauty, a wide variety of bird species charted their annual flight path for the area.

Birds nested by the thousands back then, unmolested by modern day predators like the raccoon and red fox which were brought into the area much later by European man. Marsh vegetation was pristine and productive at that time, free from the wholesale degradation of invasive plants such as salt cedar or European strains of phragmites. The shallow waters in their pristine condition were crystal clear and unaffected by schools of carp, a fish that was non-native but planted on purpose in the late 1800's. Meant to enhance native fisheries populations, the carp instead degraded water quality by stirring up mud. The resultant cloudy water blocked sunlight to valuable aquatic plants.

Geographically, the delta is located to play a strategic role in aiding the migratory path of birds flying thousands of miles north and south. Some species traverse the entire distance of North and South America as they travel from breeding to wintering areas. Weary birds, craving nutritious foods and sanctuary to replenish their depleted energy reserves, arrive after long flights. The vast marshes are a rest stop and buffet in the midst of the continent's largest desert, the Great Basin. Snowmelt, from adjacent mountains as well as the far off Uinta range, contributed to flows of the Bear River throughout its 500 mile winding channel. The mouth of this great river gently spreads across the northeast margins of the Great Salt Lake Basin and its fresh waters finally mingle with the salt-saturated waters of Great Salt Lake.

So it was: Swans, ducks, geese, pelicans, egrets, and hundreds of other species called the marshes home. And for unrecorded centuries, native Americans utilized the abundant flocks of migratory birds without diminishing their multitude or changing the character of the wetlands that the birds depended on.

The first written account of the area was from a government sponsored expedition led by John C. Fremont in 1843. He followed the Bear River channel downstream to the mystical place where the waters of the Bear River dispersed to form a giant delta and joined with the waters of Great Salt Lake. When the expedition interrupted the solitude of untold thousands of resting migratory birds, the great flocks took to the wing with an unforgettable clash that Fremont described as the "the sound of distant thunder."

In the 1850's, Mormon pioneers were sent to develop a permanent residence in the area. The abundant flocks would supply supplemental food for local families. Shooting increased substantially after the transcontinental railroad was completed in 1869. Professional hunters shot thousands of waterfowl to fill market demands. Their freshly killed ducks could be brought to the depot in Corinne and transported by rail to markets along the west coast or eastward to areas such as Denver.

Even with killing to support this commercial hunting, the marshes were able to sustain huge waterfowl populations. The remote, uncharted marshes and shallow mud flats were penetrated by very few hunters because access into the heart of the marshes was nearly impossible. With water only inches deep across hundreds of square miles of marsh and mudflat, boats could not traverse the area. So, treks into the vast wetland wilderness consisted of paddling canoes through shallow waters, then taking to foot travel with gear and supplies on the back. Soft mud would impede progress and limit the distance covered. Although hunting was unregulated, few hunters penetrated the center of the delta to disturb the huge resting flocks of waterfowl. A sort of equilibrium existed between the hunters' kill and the birds' ability to replenish the numbers taken.

That harmony was soon to change.

For farm families to survive in the desert landscape, irrigation was required to help crops and pastures grow. To that end, large scale irrigation companies were organized in the late 1800's for the purpose of diverting major flows from the Bear River onto thirsty croplands miles away from the river channel. Located upstream from the marshes, diverted flows were taken from the river to fill canals that ran across the valley to sustain an agricultural industry. During the long, hot summers so much water was taken that the river was left with only a fraction of its natural flow. The vast wetlands forming the delta of the Bear River were starved of their lifeblood. By the early 1900's, the diversions had taken their toll. The few acres of remaining wetlands were degraded and had become a breeding ground for avian botulism.

It was only a matter of time until the wetland ecosystem would come crashing down.

In 1910 disaster struck. Millions upon millions of waterfowl died, covering many thousands of acres with dead carcasses. There seemed to be no solution. In subsequent years, more die-offs occurred. The flocks were reduced to a fraction of their former numbers. Local residents were alarmed at the sudden die-off and began to seek a solution. What happened next made history.

A grassroots effort was organized to petition the U.S. Congress for establishment of a sanctuary for migratory birds. Testimony was given as to the need for a permanent bird sanctuary and rehabilitation of the marshes. Congress answered with a special bill in April of 1928, establishing Bear River Migratory Bird Refuge and appropriating sufficient funds for the project covering some 64,500 acres. In cooperation, the State of Utah donated state owned lands and granted a water right from the Bear River of 1,000 cubic feet per second. Work began immediately on a network of dikes, water control structures and administrative buildings. In 1934, after a heroic effort of construction, the refuge was declared ready for operation. It was soon to become an internationally famous haven for some 200+ species of birds.

Local residents in Brigham City threw their support behind the effort and erected a sign across main street that stands today, proclaiming Brigham City to be the "Gateway to the World's Greatest Game Bird Refuge." This was the beginning of a long partnership between the federally managed refuge and the people of the community.

What followed was termed a conservation miracle. The dry, crusted alkali flats were covered with waters once again by diverting flows from the Bear River. Dikes were built to control the depth of the water. In all, some 50 miles of dikes and diversion works enabled reclaiming more than 43,000 acres of marshes. At once, the marshes became productive and turned into a showcase for wildlife management. In order to reduce botulism outbreaks, a research laboratory was established to determine what was causing the duck disease, termed "Alkali Sickness" at the time. Within a few years, research indicated it was caused by a bacteria, not alkali in the soils as previously thought. Efforts were soon initiated to develop measures to control the die-offs.

Employees of the 1940's are credited with inventing the first airboat to traverse the shallow wetlands. Accommodation was made for the general public to visit and it soon gained the reputation as one of the world's best places to observe birdlife in natural habitats. Likewise, limited boundaries were established for public hunting and the area soon became known for the best wing shooting in the west as well. Numerous wildlife research studies were completed over the years and wildlife management techniques were developed on the area. It was truly an example of how the hand of man could successfully join with the forces of nature to replenish a degraded area. Before long, Bear River gained the unofficial status of flagship of the National Wildlife Refuge System.

Unbeknownst to anyone, the forces of nature would come into play decades later and deal a death blow to Bear River Migratory Refuge in 1984.

Ever so slowly Great Salt Lake began to rise. Record snowfalls in the mountainous watershed of the Bear River discharged flood level flows into Great Salt Lake. With no outlet to equalize the increased stream flows, the lake was driven ever higher day by day and month by month. High waters forced the Refuge to close public entry in 1984. The floodwaters continued to rise. Salt Lake levels overtopped the dike network and threatened the headquarters buildings. Circular dikes were constructed to protect numerous buildings. Floodwaters continued to rise. Finally, the lake rose to its maximum elevation in April 1987, bringing the total rise to a whopping 12 feet. Shores of Great Salt Lake expanded more than 12 miles as well. The Refuge was totally under water and every dike, building, road, tower and structure was destroyed. What floodwaters did not take down, ice flows chopped down like a giant scythe. Refuge personnel, by this time, had been transferred to other duty stations. Administration of the water-covered area was assigned to Ouray NWR, near Vernal Utah. Under their care, over flights and occasional ground visits were scheduled to ensure access gates were intact and closed. No actual land or water management was done. Use by wildlife was minimal.

Bear River Migratory Bird Refuge had gone from flagship of the National Wildlife Refuge System to being mothballed.

1988 brought an abrupt change in weather patterns; scant snowfall and anemic runoff throughout the Bear River watershed ushered in a drought cycle. With inflows dropping, Great Salt Lake elevation lowered three feet in one year alone. This prompted Regional Office supervisors in Denver to bring back one new employee to Bear River Refuge, with the primary assignment to access the condition of the Refuge and surrounding environs and propose a way forward for the future of the Refuge. Options included donating the damaged Refuge to another agency (presumably the Utah Division of Wildlife Resources) or chart a course for some degree of restoration.

At this time, the destroyed ruins of Bear River Refuge would become an opportunity for someone to take on a challenging position.

The position was officially filled in August of 1989 (by the author). Total budget for the year included salary costs and payment of fixed expenses for a small rented office of two 13'X13' rooms. A new era had begun. Now it was all about reclaiming what had taken some 55 years to build up between 1928 and 1983. The resolve of the people of Brigham City, elected officials and the U.S. Fish and Wildlife Service was about to be tested. The story that follows is unlike any other in the annals of the U.S. Fish and Wildlife Service.

I am telling this story to provide a permanent record of the incredible, unlikely accomplishment that was made by a cadre of people I consider heroes of conservation. Some were members of the community and some were employees of the Fish and Wildlife Service. Others held political offices or positions of leadership in non-governmental organizations or Universities. Together, they accomplished the *impossible* over a period of some 16 years. It required untold hours of personal investment. That is, some employees "ate, drank and slept" the business of restoring the refuge--far beyond what their paycheck reflected. Likewise, community volunteers donated untold thousands of hours and resources to assist the Refuge cause. They also made the restoration a personal cause and gave untold hours and resources toward the effort for no monetary gain whatsoever. I salute them all and am forever grateful for their dedication. I dare say, no other Refuge has a story as compelling as the restoration of Bear River. It is the shining example of a grassroots effort that did accomplish the *impossible*. After all, who would dare take on a project that involved millions of dollars of destroyed buildings, water control structures, dikes, canals and roads spread over a 100 square mile land surface? What were the people like and how did they create success? That is the personal story I want to tell so it will be permanently on record.

The account that unfolds is the tale of a community that welded itself with the Refuge staff to accomplish a task that could only be done with teamwork. I was fortunate to see that process from the inside. And now, writing from the towering platform of hindsight and the perspective that comes with twelve years of retirement, this is what I saw and experienced. I made every attempt to remain factual, albeit I had the temptation to embellish here and there. By going through the Refuge files, my journal records and personal interviews with surviving eyewitnesses, the following documentation is an accurate history. The extraordinary accomplishments are hard to believe, but what follows is a true story. It involves several steps: restoring the original Refuge habitats and facilities; enhancing the water management system; expanding the land holdings; and finally, constructing the Education Center.

May all those who contributed to the effort be recognized for what they did.

CHAPTER 1

THE MELTING POT
OF PHILOSOPHIES

I didn't think I was arrogant; I certainly had no intention to be, but I just thought volunteers were inferior to regular paid employees. I thought they were less motivated, less skilled and less experienced than *real* employees. Was I ever in for an education.

Unbeknownst to me, my errant viewpoint was about to be shattered by a string of events starting in 1990. Volunteers from the Brigham City community were about to enlighten my simple, erroneous notion and write a new chapter in the history of Bear River Migratory Bird Refuge.

First, a little about my management style and philosophy. The U.S. Fish and Wildlife Service gives their refuge managers tremendous latitude in management activities and style. It's not necessarily intended, but it just happens because supervisory personnel are a long way away (my case Denver, Colorado) and they have numerous refuges and programs to supervise. This means supervisors are lucky to physically visit an individual refuge more than once a year. Sometimes less than that. As a result, managers run their operations with minimal intervention unless they create a problem that requires Regional Office attention. It was about as close to being unsupervised as you can get in civil service.

Being left alone was good news for me. I most enjoyed managing in my own *grey zone*, where I interpreted policy, or more correctly, set my own policy as much as possible. I believed my mission was to get the most done for wildlife. Rules usually just got in the way of progress and had to be bent (or broken) to improve efficiency and get the most done with limited dollars. I broke plenty of rules, regulations and policies; but I always made sure it resulted in more getting done on the ground. Most importantly, I made sure good records were kept of all funds we spent, so they could be tracked to an end product. Since it was my neck on the line, other staff and volunteers generally enjoyed the free-wheeling atmosphere to just get the job done.

For example, I once violated national contracting procedures by going around a pre-awarded supply contract for ATV's. This contract was awarded on the national level and *theoretically* was the cheapest price available. We were required to purchase off this contract. It seemed like a high price to me, so I loaded my trade-in ATV and drove to Big Boys Toys in Ogden and asked what they could do. To my delight, they offered me a deal that saved $500 over the National bid. I went ahead and purchased the new ATV without asking for special authorization or letting Regional Office personnel know what I was up to. I reasoned they would surely tell me no if I asked for permission.

One fine day several weeks later, I received a call from the finance office in Denver and the person on the other end of the line was extremely agitated. It was made abundantly clear that I had committed an illegal purchase and that I was potentially in a lot of trouble. I remained calm as I got my posterior chewed every which way. It is always a good idea to let someone vent and dump all over you when you are obviously in the wrong. After being totally quiet for what seemed like forever, I finally took the chance to say something. I explained as gently as possible that it would be a shame if the public found out that I was being reprimanded for saving the government money. There was a little more grousing, then the phone call ended abruptly with a hang-up on the other end. That was the last I ever heard of the matter.

The moral to the story is this: government procedure is often less efficient and more costly, so work around it however you can.

On another occasion, I needed some basic office furniture like cabinets and bookshelves. It just so happened that a moratorium had been placed on purchasing furniture because some high ranking official, probably in Washington D.C., had made some extravagant purchases. I needed something basic, but policy said I needed Washington Office approval. That was going to be a long time in coming, and it would require miles of "red tape." So, I worked around the system in a two step scheme by first purchasing some lumber on a purchase order, then after some time had lapsed I hired a local cabinet maker to fabricate what I needed (step two). The cabinet makers cost was lower because he was using lumber I provided. He agreed to bill me without using the term "furniture" so it would not tip off the regulators in the Regional Office. The cabinet company could have cared less about tweaking the wording of what I needed the work to be called as long as he got paid. Everything was going according to plan until he finished the bookcases and cabinets and decided to deliver them to my office. He must have been thinking it would be a pleasant surprise. In this case, it was not a pleasant surprise. Two regional office employees were on site doing a financial audit, an activity that is a very rare occurrence. They were going through our records with a fine tooth comb looking for anything they could find that was out of financial policy. I was feeling really good about the way we had hidden our numerous "shortcuts" and our records seemed to be squeaky clean. They were about to complete their audit when things went South for me. Really South.

Out of nowhere, a delivery truck from the cabinet shop appeared and backed up to the front door. There was no ignoring this situation, the truck's back-up alarm was sounding a loud beep, beep, beep as if to announce its arrival. I couldn't believe what I was seeing. I was horrified and wanted to shout "go away! Not now!!" Two smiling men began carrying in the illegally purchased furniture in full view of the Regional inspectors. I watched with my jaw dropped in disbelief that this could be happening at the exact wrong moment. I thought to myself, "why couldn't this have happened tomorrow?"

There I was BUSTED. The two inspectors looked at me and asked what in the world did I think I was doing. I knew it was time to just lay out the simple truth. I told them I was trying to work around the Washington moratorium on furniture so I bought lumber with one purchase order and had the furniture constructed with another purchase order (illegal), then I wrote it up as something other than furniture (illegal again).

They looked at me in disbelief, and I just stood there waiting for the guilty verdict. They shook their heads and said some things about the whole process being illegal. With no further discussion about the matter, they returned to Denver. I was a nervous wreck for weeks because I was sure they were going to report back to headquarters and decide on the appropriate punishment. To my delighted surprise, I never heard a word back. There was no nasty phone call or no registered letter of reprimand. It was as if they never saw anything! I was afraid to broach the subject later on with their office, so I never asked about it. The moral to this story is this: when you are doing the best you can and accomplishing the mission, your "reasonable" indiscretions may be overlooked-at least sometimes.

Some Regional Office supervisors in those days were cut from a different cloth than what you may encounter today. They were "old school" managers who had learned earlier in their careers how to manage refuge lands on a shoe-string budget. They were highly motivated to do the most they could simply for the sake of wildlife. They were willing to stick their necks out and operate outside protocol to get something done. Administration and red tape was less important than the mission of managing wildlife. They tended to overlook some rules if it helped get the job done.

Along those lines, I was fortunate to have Barney Schrank as my immediate supervisor. He was impressed when something got done and did not concern himself with trying to reign me in even though he knew I was regularly ignoring some regulations. On occasions when it was evident I did not follow protocol, he would say to me "I know nothing." His grin communicated that he was pleased with the work, yet pretending to believe I had followed the approved process. I was grateful for his support. To this day I have very fond memories of our working relationship.

When you add my willingness to move ahead and skirt around "red tape" for the sake of progress and Barney's willingness to over-look my indiscretions, the result was that we made some real progress.

All in all, the stage was set for some unusual accomplishment when the volunteer staff began to jell. We soon developed an atmo-sphere of trust and dedication to a shared goal and vision for the future of the Refuge. The volunteers would devote a full measure of their time and talents and I would do likewise. Their personal and voluntary dedication was met with my management style to stick my neck out to help them make the most of their efforts. Those were great days. It was *us* working on the restoration of the Refuge. We were "all in."

In 1989, I had no comprehension of what marvelous things were ahead and what lifetime memories were about to be made.

CHAPTER 2

WHERE IS BEAR RIVER?

I had been stationed at Rainwater Basin Wetland Management District for nearly 12 years and I was beginning to feel the itch to move to something new. Our home in Kearney, Nebraska was truly a page out of the mid-America play book. My duties were spread across 7 counties on 42 separate Waterfowl Production Areas. Home life was great, with Kearney being a small, but progressive college town. My three kids were getting a good education in a wholesome setting. Hunting and fishing was good. Kathy, my wife, was more than happy with her surroundings as well. Still, I felt that urge to take on something different -a new challenge.

My opportunity came when the application period was opened for the Refuge Manager position at Bear River Migratory Bird Refuge. Wow, I thought that would be a great job, but I did not let myself get too excited because I knew lots of managers more senior than myself would be throwing their hat in the ring. But my first concern was to get Kathy to agree to the application. After some thought, I came up with the perfect approach. Since she really wanted to stay in Kearney, I said it would be a good idea for me to apply for Bear River because I, for sure, would NOT get the job. And by applying, it would help my argument for staying in Kearney because I could point to the fact that I was really looking and applying for jobs.

I called the Brigham City Chamber of Commerce and had them send out a packet of information, which we looked over one evening as I made out the application for Refuge Manager. When I mailed off the application, the whole issue went to the back of my mind. I knew that eventually, probably months away, I would get notice of who was selected for the job -someone besides me of course.

After a number of months, I began to wonder why the selection had not been announced. Just for curiosity's sake, I gave the selecting official, Barney Schranck, a call to find out what was going on. I am glad I was sitting down. I really thought Keith Hansen, a great refuge manager who even had prior experience at Bear River, would get the nod. Instead, Barney said he had made the selection but it was not approved by the Regional Director yet. Then I got a little light headed when he asked if I could keep a secret. "I selected you," he said, "and I'm sure it will go through ok; but you can't say a word till it's official." For the first few seconds I was elated, then I wondered how I was going to tell Kathy and the kids I was selected for a job I told them I was not going to get.

Kathy and the kids had long forgotten that I had a job application in the mill. It had been around 5 months. Working up the nerve after I got home, I announced that I was very fortunate to have been selected for Refuge Manager at Bear River. It went over like a lead balloon. Chad, our mild mannered 16 year old son, yelled out some defiant word for the first time in his life. Ryan, at 12 years old just became stressed out and Amy at 7 years seemed to take it ok. Kathy, on the other hand, had a look of horror on her face. Ok. This was going to be a hard sell. When Kathy could speak, she said "you weren't supposed to get that job.". Then she asked, "Where is Bear River anyway?" We got out a map and after some time located Brigham City. Nobody was impressed. This was going to prove to be a hard move to make.

Between all the issues of a permanent move, I started to get some information about Bear River Migratory Bird Refuge. Most encouraging was news of a $3Million earmark for restoring the refuge. That sounded huge: I had never dealt with that much money before. I was also told that everything had been destroyed and a small rental office in town would be waiting for me when I arrived in August.

We were allowed a house hunting trip, so a few weeks later Kathy and I flew into Salt Lake City and drove north to Brigham City for the first time. After our house hunting, we drove out West Forest street to the Refuge. What a sight. Nothing but bare ground and piles of rubble where the headquarters use to be. I was at a loss as to what the way forward would be for this mess.

So in August of 1989, we packed up everything and made the big move, arriving in Brigham City just before school started. We jammed the family into a kitchenette in the Galaxy Inn- that is along with two black lab dogs. That turned out to be a very long 3 weeks before moving into our new home.

My first day of work amounted to me walking across the motel parking lot and into a strip mall where I had keys to a depressing little office. It amounted to two small rooms measuring 13 feet square. I got the door opened and found two desks stacked together and a couple chairs. No phone, no computer, no windows, no employees. After looking around, I pulled a chair in front of a desk and propped my feet up. Leaning back with my hands folded behind my neck and staring at a blank wall, I asked out loud "well Trout my boy, what are we going to do now?"

CHAPTER 3

ONE APPROACH TO REFUGE MANAGEMENT- WINNING AT THE MANAGEMENT GAME

Hundreds of National Wildlife Refuges are spread across the American landscape in all sorts of diverse places. Since they are located in areas that have special wildlife values, most are in remote spots that have not been ruined by human development -at least not yet. Remote, rural settings lend themselves to a feeling of independence from agency control and supervision. It is not that individual refuge managers have a negative attitude toward regional or central office (Washington) supervision; it is just that their far flung location makes it difficult for off-site administrators to fully understand all the local issues. Refuge managers become independent thinkers by necessity. They learn to take charge and make decisions in order to get the job done. Many issues that cross a refuge manager's desk on a daily basis need to be dealt with and resolved quickly. They can't wait weeks or months for the chain of command to mull over a solution. So, any good refuge manager learns early on to take calculated risks and make the decisions necessary to keep the ball rolling. That is just part of the job. I loved it.

By the time I reached Bear River Migratory Bird Refuge, I had nearly 10 years of experience as a manager. Operating without immediate oversight was just fine with me. I knew, or thought I knew, how far I could divert from normal protocol and still get away with it. A delicate balance had to be reached if anything was to get done. Some rules had to be followed, but, by the same token, some had to be ignored. There were other rules to bend until they were hardly recognizable. Sometimes, a rule made higher up the chain of command just did not fit in every diverse location. Surviving the role of Refuge Manager, meant finding a comfort zone and operating within it. Usually, the more freewheeling and extreme, the more jobs get completed. It was a simple matter of making as many common sense moves as possible without getting called on the carpet.

My experience had molded me into a manager who was comfortable with operating in the *grey zone* to accomplish more than those going strictly by all the regulations and policies.

My one-of-a-kind supervisor, Larry Shanks, once explained it this way " There three kinds of government employees: 1) Those who have to be dragged along by the rule book; 2) Those who follow the book; and 3) Those who are out front of the book and rewrite it for themselves." Larry was definitely out front and I liked to think of myself as being out front with him. I will comment more about Larry later on when he played a critical role in the Education Center funding.

There is one other principle when working for the government. When you want something done quickly, never ask for permission because the answer will be "no" or "wait." If you are a manager worth your salt, you have to stick your neck out and make the decision and be ready to take the fallout. It has been said, "it is easier to ask for forgiveness than to ask for permission." I think well paid leaders need to make common sense decisions at times, regardless of what *the book* says.

In addition to operating loosely within the network of rules, I empowered my staff to do the jobs they were hired to do. There were times when I should have supervised more closely, but for the most part my staff gave exceptional effort and worked together well. They made me look good. The staff was in a constant state of evolution because we added new employees throughout the years and the Refuge landscape was also developing continually. I was usually over my head because so many new things were coming along as we developed the Refuge. We were anything but stagnant, and that brought an air of excitement with each day.

We were an out of the mold staff and had a reputation for getting the job done. I enjoyed that and I think the staff did too. The staff generally worked as a team and they even liked being together outside work hours. Frequently, on weekends or holidays, they would get together for parties in their homes. We also took hunting or camping trips together. Some say leaders should not socialize with their staff. All I can say is that it worked in our case.

CHAPTER 4

BAD NEWS FROM THE REGIONAL OFFICE-WHAT DO WE DO NOW

Our first glimpse of Brigham City came with a house hunting trip in July 1989, a month before we were to enter on duty at the Refuge. Everything was new and unfamiliar. The steel arch over Main Street grabbed my attention. It read, "Welcome to Brigham City, Home of the World's Greatest Gamebird Refuge." We booked a room in the Howard Johnson Motel on the south side of town with the intent of spending several days with a realtor searching for a home. I resisted the urge to go look at the Refuge because I knew it would suck me in and I would not be able to concentrate on house hunting. So, one thing at a time. After several days, we located a home for sale privately and made a deal. Now I could shift attention and go take a look at the Refuge. At this point I didn't even know how to get there! So, I asked a local, "How do you get to the Refuge?" I was told to go west on Forest Street and follow it 14 miles to the end, so off we went.

After several miles of pavement the road turned to gravel. From smooth gravel it went to potholes and gravel. From potholes and gravel it went to a blend of dirt, potholes and patches of gravel. Threading the rental car back and forth along the road/trail for a number of miles, we viewed a landscape that was devoid of all vegetation and covered with a layer of alkali like nothing I had ever seen. It was impossible for me to imagine this as a former marshland sustaining large numbers of birds. Sunset was nearing on that hot summer's day when we finally arrived at a locked gate across the road, just a few hundred yards from the old headquarters site. I got out of the car and walked around the gate to take in the sight.

The hot summer air was filled with a salty stench, an unfamiliar aroma for my nostrils. In front of me stretched a barren, utterly flat landscape. Front and center was the old headquarters site that was now a cluster of rubble piles. One pile was the office, one pile the Visitor Center. Other piles included the employee residences and shop. I was standing near the channel of the Bear River; immediately to the north was the ruins of the bridge which crossed two channels of the river. It carried vehicles continuously from the early 1930's until the great flood. Now it was reduced to wreckage from the forces of a shifting ice pack knocking the concrete decks off their abutments. The 100 foot steel tower, itself a symbol of the Refuge, was gone. It was smashed flat to the ground by those same forces of nature.

I spent a few minutes walking around in the heat and putrid air. Everything was broken, even the steel water control gates on the bridge abutments. They were completely mangled into useless scrap. I had never been on a refuge, anywhere, and felt the despair that was sinking into my psyche. Here was 100 square miles of barren wasteland. Over 70 years of work by untold numbers of people had been erased by a flood event that the area had not experienced in a century. Kathy joined me as we walked through the rubble back to the car. Could this place be brought back to its former condition? How long would it take? What kind of funding would it require? My thoughts were not in a good place as we made the long slow drive back to Brigham City. I wondered," would my time here be a big waste?"

So, to sum it up. The Refuge was closed to the public. The access road was nearly impassable. No water management was being done, nor was it possible. All water control structures (about 50 total) were damaged and inoperable. The 50 mile dike network was damaged beyond use. Interior access roads on top of the dikes were washed out. Supply canals were silted in. Every single building was destroyed and reduced to rubble. It was a bleak picture. About the only good news was the Salt Lake had dropped a full 3 feet from its peak flooding elevation. It appeared the flooding was over for good. At least that was one thing we could hope for.

The next day, Kathy and I returned home in Kearney, Nebraska to spend the next month packing up our belongings and saying goodbye to the friends we had made during our 12 years there. Our toughest job would be preparing our three children for their new lives in a culture totally new to them. Chad would enter into the 11th grade, Ryan into 7th and Amy into 3rd. Each of our children would feel some degree of trauma, but Ryan would have the roughest period of adjustment. I always regretted the pain my family had to go through because of the moves I made through my career.

Our permanent move occurred on August 17, 1989, Kathy's 40 birthday. We had about two weeks before school started and we were due to take possession of our home on Labor Day weekend. We ended up being jammed into a kitchenette motel room with three kids and two lab dogs for a couple of weeks. Not earthshaking, but it left an unpleasant memory that won't go away! I still can't figure out why I didn't drive a few miles to Ogden and rent a decent room for my traumatized family.

It was a very short commute on my first official day of work. I walked out of the motel room and about 100 feet straight across a parking lot into a strip mall. My office had been pre- arranged by Regional Office personnel and amounted to two small and claustrophobic rooms. No windows and no glass door. Just two poorly lit, isolated rooms unmarked and very basic. When I first saw the office, it was *hate at first sight.* Since I was the only employee, I opened the door turned on the light and pulled up a chair in front of a grey metal government desk. No computer, no phone, no radio and nobody to talk to. I sat there a moment then kicked my feet up onto the desk and leaned back in the chair. With my hands clasped behind my neck I began talking to myself. I said, *"Al my boy, what are we going to do now?"* That was the official conversation I had with myself as my lonely career at Bear River Migratory Bird Refuge began.

My next *official* duty was to visit the local Fred Meyer store and buy a telephone so I could call Barney Schranck, my immediate supervisor in Denver and tell him I was on duty (note: those were pre cell phone years). Barney and I got along extremely well and he was doing everything he could to get me some support. However, he soon had to give me some very bad news. The budget request of several million dollars specifically for Bear River Migratory Bird Refuge recovery had been removed from the budget by someone on the president's staff. Barney informed me that no other funding source would be forthcoming. It appeared that the administration did not think Bear River Migratory Bird Refuge needed **any** funding to fix the flood damage! That news hit me hard. How was I going to get anything done? And worse yet, it looked like the administration didn't care. This was a gut punch.

I was left with only one alternative: get out and meet people and hopefully generate some political support for future funding. That was something I had no experience with. All I could do was try my best. Nothing else was happening.

CHAPTER 5

WHAT HAVE YOU GOT TO LOSE?

There I was, the "new kid on the block," having transferred into Utah without any prior knowledge of Bear River Migratory Bird Refuge, the landscape or the Brigham City community. I was totally disconnected and just trying to become basically familiar with my surroundings. I entered on duty in August; by October it was evident the deck was stacked against anything happening for a long time. My budget was minimal: it included only enough to cover rent, utilities, my salary and a few basic supplies. There was no prospect of funding for any cleanup or construction on the Refuge. I was alone without promise of any other staff. It looked pretty bleak to say the least.

The solution was crystal- clear in my mind. All I needed was a very large special appropriation. It would take multiple millions to do all the construction and rehabilitation necessary to bring the Refuge back into operation. There was a lot of work to do and an entire staff to hire. Anything short of a hefty appropriation was just not going to help. Or so I thought.

I had spent the month of September contacting City, County and State officials. I also visited Utah State University College of Natural Resources and met some lead professors. I was getting involved with

Bear River Water Development meetings being held monthly in the State Capital building. There I met dozens of political officials, agency directors and people associated with conservation organizations in a somewhat contentious atmosphere of planning for the construction of dams on the main channel of the Bear River above the Refuge. Overall, I met lots of people who voiced support of the Refuge, but no one had solutions or even offered help. At this point I was a glorified public relations man, but I was not getting anything done on the Refuge.

Then one fateful day in October my world was about to be shaken. My career was about to take a turn into what was uncharted water for me. Little did I know that I was about to be stretched in areas of my professional career that were beyond my imagination and comfort zone.

It started late one Friday afternoon when I was having a conversation with a Box Elder County Commissioner in my little "cracker box" office. I hope you remember that I hated that office with a passion. Anyway, without a knock, the door burst open and a short man with an assertive voice interrupted by asking for the Refuge Manager. I introduced myself and he told me his name was Bob Ebeling and he wanted a job. My goal was to get rid of this guy as quickly as possible. First off, I didn't have funding for any staff, and secondly I would not have hired him even if I did. He just seemed "wrong" for the job, he did not fit the mold of a typical maintenance man and he was too old anyway (mid 60's). I mean he was ancient, and we all know old people have nothing to contribute (cool off, I'm just kidding).

I wanted him discouraged quickly and out of my office so I could finish my "more important" conversation with the County Commissioner. I started telling him I had no funding for a position and that my agency had not even approved the concept of additional staff. He started waving his hands in front of my face in a gesture for me to stop talking. Then he fired back, I don't want pay I want to volunteer for two years so we can restore the Refuge. His offer fell on my deaf ears. Not only was he taking up my valuable time, now he wants even more of my time if he comes back as a volunteer.

As dumb as it may sound now, at that point in my career I had a very low opinion of volunteers. I had never seen an example of volunteers accomplishing anything very big. Oh sure, they could get your mail, or clean your office or maybe even paint something (small). But, I reasoned that volunteers could not even begin to make a dent in the size and scope of the projects we were faced with. So there we stood, me with a rotten attitude and Bob looking me in the eye for an answer. I fumbled around to find the words and said something along the lines that I would call him back if I could use him.

That evening over supper, I was recounting my daily highlights with Kathy. I got to the part with Bob asking to volunteer and Kathy asked, "What did you tell him?" "I said I would call him back so I could get rid of him" was my reply. Kathy looked a little puzzled and suggested I give him a chance. She asked, "What do you have to lose?" Her wisdom spoke through my thick head and prideful attitude. What did I have to lose? The answer was nothing whatsoever.

I gave Bob a call that evening and said, "Meet me on Monday morning at 8:00 in the office." Sure enough, Bob arrived right on time that next Monday and greeted me with the energetic declaration "Good morning Boss!" and from that moment on a new page was turned for my career and the Refuge restoration. He immediately unloaded, with exuberant energy, his vision of restoring the Refuge to public use by the next 4th of July -9 months away. He could hardly contain himself as he detailed the steps to make it happen. I didn't fully believe he could do it, but I was impressed with his energy and attitude and knew it would at least help. Besides, I needed his "can do" attitude for encouragement.

This guy's energy was **impressive**. I have always been on the over-energetic side, but Bob was over the top. He exuded ideas and plans for the Refuge like I couldn't believe. Come to find out, Bob was a retired "project engineer" from Thiokol Corporation. This was the company located on the northern shore of Great Salt Lake and is most known for building rocket boosters for the space shuttle. Bob had worked his way up the organization into a supervisory role over a staff of engineers. At the pinnacle of his career, Bob had some sway over giving approvals to NASA for launching space shuttle flights. One flight changed his career and affected him for the rest of his life. When NASA requested permission to launch the *Challenger* on a cold winter morning, Bob strongly opposed giving approval. However, his suggestion to delay the launch was overridden by the General Manager. Thiokol gave an official OK and the ensuing explosion in flight tipped his world upside down. The stress and guilt affected his health and he eventually retired right before I arrived in August of 1989. Bob deeply loved the Refuge and wanted to pour his energy totally into the restoration so he could put the past behind and move ahead into a new phase of life. Bob was highly respected by his peers for his career work and well known around town. It also needs to be mentioned that he was a man of faith in Jesus and he lived his faith daily. You could say "He was the real deal."

That first morning when Bob arrived for "work", I quickly realized he was going to be a huge asset. I couldn't help but to whisper a prayer of thanks to God for dumping this fireball of a guy right in my lap. Knowing this was a big break for me, I took out an extra key to the office and handed it to Bob. "This makes you my assistant manager," I said while handing it to him. I told him I had to concentrate most of my efforts in trying to get funding, so he could put most of his efforts into on-the-ground projects. We pulled an old gray government desk next to mine in our little room and within a few days we bought him a telephone as well. The energy and talent of Bob Ebeling would soon be focused on the Refuge. I was about to experience something new and exciting. My career would never be the same.

CHAPTER 6

IGNITING THE SPARK

After I had declared Bob my official assistant (actually, there was nothing "official" about it) he filled the job perfectly. I was glad to have the companionship and encouragement that he brought to the workplace. He arrived *every* morning full of energy and ideas. We truly enjoyed each other's personality and we had one other dimension that welded us together at the hip. Bob had what I would call a rough and tumble life in his early years. He lived hard, played hard and I am told he also drank hard at times. By the time I met Bob, he had left all that behind and declared Jesus as his Lord and Savior. He prayed frequently and held on to the truths of the Bible. I was also in that same faith, so we struck it off from "top to bottom" you might say. When we started the day, the first few minutes were reserved for a prayer between the two of us. We poured our hearts out before the Lord and asked for his guidance and blessings. It was a unique season in my career and I cherish the memories.

When we joined forces, it brought a unique and effective mix of talents. Being an experienced employee of the U.S. Fish and Wildlife Service, I had knowledge of the ways the bureaucracy ran and what it required. Bob, on the opposite side of the scale came from private industry and was molded by the early days of the U.S. space program with its lofty goals and tight deadlines. He knew how to get things done. Bob was a man with goals he wanted to accomplish each day, week, month and year. He had an incredible level of focus. One other critical and effective element was his dedication to the Refuge. He was ALL IN. He gave his time without reservation -24/7. He gave money, supplies, vehicles and tools. He owned a boat and donated its unlimited use. As Bob demonstrated his level of commitment on a daily basis, his recruitment and fundraising efforts were successful. He talked the talk and walked the walk.

His first act of recruitment was to get a retired contractor, Wayne Jensen. Wayne had connections in the contracting world and was himself a man who was use to getting things done. He helped Bob refine some construction plans as the scope of Refuge restoration was being evaluated.

Bob identified the first major restoration goal -opening the historic 12 mile auto tour route to the public by July 4, 1990. That task, I thought, was out of the question since we had no funding or resources to rejuvenate 12 miles of roadway and the bridge across the Bear River. The route also contained numerous water control structures that required guardrails for vehicles as well as catwalks and flashboards to effectively manage water.

Bob took action by tackling the first major problem. We had no access to the 50 mile network of dikes because the floodwaters had eroded the dikes and they were impassable. Bob's solution was to contact Rick Whitaker who was partial owner of Whitaker Construction. I accompanied Bob out of church one Sunday and watched him "put the touch" on Rick in the parking lot. Bob's approach was a bit humorous because it was so direct, really the kind of request that was outrageous on one hand but asked in a way that expected a "yes." Bob asked for a road grader to blade the main dikes enough for vehicle travel.

He said it was for the volunteers to get their work done. Nothing was mentioned about the government. Rick agreed, right there on the spot, to donate a grader and operator if Bob could get the fuel donated by someone else. They shook hands on the deal and off we went. Bob next lined up a donation of gravel and purchased enough fuel with cash donations. His immediate efforts yielded $13,000 in donations, enough to get a good start in those waning days in the fall of 1989.

One *problem* that came up immediately was how to manage donations and give the donors a tax exemption. Bob's solution was to call his growing band of volunteers "Friends of the Refuge" and then have the Box Elder Wildlife Federation (an organization with tax exempt status) handle the money in a special account. How simple! Bob had people make out their checks to Box Elder Wildlife Federation and on the memo line put Friends of the Refuge. It was probably not very legal, but who cares. The Federation enjoyed the extra energy the Friends brought to their organization. Some members of the Federation also donated and joined the Friends as well. It would be years later when the Friends of Bear River Refuge would be legally established and go on to fund the Education Center. That part of the story is told later on.

Another early donation that helped get the ball rolling was a truck load of 2x6 dimensional lumber the volunteers needed to build flashboards for water control structures. These flashboards are critical for impounding river flows and holding the marshes at the proper depth. Lining up the donated lumber was one thing, but we had no place for volunteers to process the lumber to length, cleat the boards together and install hooks for installation. Solution. Bob paid a visit to an old friend, Ruben Dietz. Ruben was a long time employee of the Utah Division of Wildlife Resources and later manager of the Bear River Club. At the time, Ruben managed Indian School properties for some out of state landlords. When Bob asked Ruben to give the volunteers the FREE use of a shop building and for Ruben's company to pay all the utilities, I was braced for a "no." Surprise! Ruben agreed and the Friends suddenly had a shop building to operate from. It seemed to me that Bob was successful at garnering donations because he expected other people to join his example. This was **his** project and Bob was leading the effort. His boldness was born out of dedication and focus. Everyone knew he was giving it his all without being paid. He was giving it his full time effort from the heart.

When Anderson Lumber delivered the 2X6's, Bob lined up a work shift of volunteers to fabricate the flashboards. All saws, drills and hand tools were brought by the volunteers themselves. Bob's goal was to have the flashboards ready to install when the spring run-off of 1990 arrived, and he was right on schedule!

With all this happening, there was an air of excitement about the Refuge. More and more volunteers were showing up as word of mouth spread. I went to a Brigham City Council meeting one evening to just introduce myself and give them an update on the Refuge. After my presentation, I received a round of applause from the city council and some of the public also attending. One councilman pulled his checkbook from his back pocket (back in the day people actually used checks rather than cards) and made a personal donation in front of everyone.

I was starting to love Brigham City and feel right at home. I knew in my heart that whether or not the Fish and Wildlife Service was going along with this, WE WERE ON OUR WAY. I did not report the day to day progress to my superiors in the Fish and Wildlife Service. I knew that the bureaucracy would have problems with every step they were taking and poison the enthusiasm of all the volunteers by slowing them down with regulations. Believe me, there are regulations that are against almost everything you do to get a job done quickly.

CHAPTER 7

PUTTING THE
FUTURE ON PAPER

While the corps of volunteers under the direction of Bob Ebeling were making strides on the Refuge, I was busy with some administrative hurdles. The primary challenge I faced was making the work of the volunteers legitimate in the eyes of the bureaucracy. All projects need to fall under the umbrella of an approved plan of some kind.

Bear River Refuge needed to have a comprehensive plan before it could move forward in the budget process, or even have volunteer work recognized as beneficial. One problem was, I hated plans. I hated writing plans and I hated being constrained by plans. I believed that plans only got in the way and slowed down common sense decisions. As you can imagine, with such a bad attitude it was going to be very hard for me to step aside from the excitement of on-the-ground work to write a plan. I also need to say that our outfit (along with most government agencies) tend to over plan every action. I had seen too many plans become obsolete before they were even approved. Starting out with such a rotten attitude was going to make this process a real challenge for me. Never-the-less, it had to be done.

In our case, the plan was going to be under the Environmental Assessment process. ICK. In reality it would take over a year and engage the Regional Office (in Denver) as well as the local populace through at least two public meetings (they never go well). I received approval to hire one employee who could serve as the principal author. What a waste of good manpower I thought, spending that much money only to write up a plan and not really doing anything on the ground. The person most suited to do this kind of job was a man who had recently retired near Logan and was familiar with the Refuge. Keith Hansen was a former refuge manager and was well respected for judgment and management skills. I decided to look him up and see if he wanted to take on the task as a rehired annuant. To my delight, Keith agreed to do the job. Keith did not disappoint me: his experience and work ethic to complete the plan was a huge benefit to the effort. Over the next two years, Keith wrote, and rewrote the plan until it was ready for Regional Director approval.

Some major hurdles included two public meetings. They were held in the high school auditorium and attended by hundreds of concerned citizens. I was nervous that the crowd would go ugly. It was from my years in North Dakota, South Dakota and Nebraska where refuge issues ran at odds with the local farming mentality. I was imagining the opposition being organized through the Farm Bureau and blocking our plans to rebuild the Refuge. I had underestimated Bob Ebeling and the corps of volunteers that he organized to the smallest detail.

The first public meeting was to involve me giving a summary status of the Refuge and allow anyone from the public to make a recorded comment as to their opinion on what should happen to the Refuge. Anyone could say whatever they wanted, even if it was dumb. We were supposed to analyze those comments and develop a long range plan for the Refuge. The value of this meeting was to help identify all issues involved in Refuge restoration. Knowing all the issues would hopefully make our long range plan better. However, I had never seen this process go smoothly. Someone in the crowd would usually go off on some pet peeve and get a string of gripes going.

Bob was not about to let the meeting go forward without his hand of guidance. Anticipating some negative comments, he "stacked the deck" during the comment period by having his handpicked Refuge supporters sprinkled throughout the list of people who had signed up to make comments. Bob said if someone made a negative comment, a Refuge friend would follow-up with comments to neutralize it. I was overjoyed. What other Refuge would have enough local support to host a public meeting stacked in their favor. Nobody from Refuges that I ever knew.

As you can imagine, the meeting came off very well. The vast majority of comments were positive and we had a list of issues to address while we formulated our long range plan. Bob led off with public comments and set the stage on a positive note. The discussions that night were more like a love-in than a typical government gripe session. I came away supercharged, thanks to my wonderful support group.

Our plan took shape quickly. It proposed three steps. Step one was to restore the original water management system with its 50 water control structures and 50 miles of dikes. Step two was to enhance the "old" system with an additional 50 miles of dikes and another 50 water control structures. Then step three was to expand the Refuge by purchasing private land as well as wetland easements. Step 3 also included the construction of a visitor center and headquarters facility to make the "new and improved" Refuge fully functional for the visiting public.

Our next job was to identify the exact boundaries of lands we wanted to purchase outright (fee title) and lands we wanted to protect through purchase of an easement from the landowner. I knew putting those boundaries on paper would become a contentious issue. Utah is

80% Federal land, and I knew any proposal to purchase private land was going to hit opposition. Still, we forged ahead with identifying lands important to the future of the Refuge. I had an uneasy feeling in my gut as the acreage in the plan added up.

The next year would be highlighted by volunteers working under the direction of Bob Ebleling and Keith Hansen working behind the scenes completing his long range refuge plan (termed Ecological Assessment).

CHAPTER 8

MOVING AHEAD WITHOUT AUTHORIZATION

Late Winter of 1990 found Bob Ebleling busy lining up the resources he would need to have the Refuge reopened to the public by July 4th and to have the 5 main impoundments holding fresh water from the Bear River. Both goals were a reach. The impoundments were inoperable due to damage to the diversion structures and dikes. Each unit alone was an average of 5,000 surface acres and designed to hold 20,000 acre/feet of water. Bob was not to be discouraged. Consider also that opening the public tour route meant repairing 12 miles of roads and numerous bridges over water control structures. For starters, the main bridge at the old headquarters site consisted of sixteen concrete decks that were knocked into the river channel by a massive ice flow during the flood. Most normal people with any sense would have found a good reason to back away from this challenge. Failure was highly probable; so I thought.

Bob never flinched at the challenge before him. Instead he was busy putting together a fraternity of people who loved the Refuge and embraced the same restoration goals. The corps of volunteers were successful people in their former careers. Some were managers, administrators, production workers, engineers and scientists. Most were newly retired and had a *thing* about giving back to the community. It was, in my opinion, partly a generational value system. They had prospered and now they felt it was their responsibility to return some of their good fortune to the country and its citizens. Those volunteers exhibited a sense of duty. I was blown away. Lasting friendships developed among many of those people. Their love for the Refuge cut across the boundaries of social status, politics, religion and professions.

So, with about 50 volunteers Bob organized cleanup efforts at first to get rid of the rubble at headquarters and at the main diversions around the Reeder and Whistler headgates. Tom Walker, a newly retired engineer from Thiokol, volunteered to remove the damaged steel radial gates and actuators at headquarters. Brent Christensen, another local citizen, volunteered to use his personally owned backhoe to clear out the debris at the Reeder canal structure. Once dug from the channel, it was loaded and hauled away in privately owned trucks.

Golden Spike National Historic Site, about 30 miles north, became aware of the volunteer efforts and transferred a dozer as "excess federal property" to the Refuge so it could be used to help the cleanup effort. It was our first piece of equipment and we were thrilled. Here, once again, I had to ignore Service policy requiring all operators to receive heavy equipment certification prior to using the machine. Heck, I thought to myself, what could possibly go wrong if we just used good judgment. Lucky for me no one had an accident—well, I should say nothing was reported to me.

By now I was fully comfortable with the skills and abilities of the volunteers so I just let them go. I felt that they were on a roll and should not be slowed down by little things like government policy. Just imagine how long it would take to get official approval to reuse or repair bridge decking (believe me, a loooong time). You would need clearance through Regional Office Safety people. Regional or

Washington D.C. Engineering would feel the need to inspect, evaluate and approve/disapprove all structural work. Just me asking would bring up huge "red flags" and stop all work until who knows when. I chose to let the volunteers run with their abilities. I would report the volunteer activities as accomplishments after they were done. My boss Barney Schranck, to his credit, could tell something special was happening and he let it go. I was comfortable with taking the fall if something happened and so I did not get Barney involved, thereby reducing his risk of liability in my schemes here at the Refuge. Barney was good with that and would often say "I know nothing." I was good with that, so we worked well together.

By far, the most dangerous and largest project in 1990 was repairing the bridge spanning the mouth of the Bear River. This bridge provided the only crossing of the Bear River channel and gave access to a major part of the Refuge. It served the dual purpose of regulating water flows via large steel control gates mounted between each of the abutments. It was the heart of both the water control and road systems. Ice flows had done incredible damage by lifting the heavy concrete bridge decks off their abutments and dropping them into the river channel. These concrete slabs were two lanes wide and roughly 25 feet long. Likewise, the system of steel water control gates were damaged beyond repair and would have to be lifted out of their resting place by a crane and removed off site.

Repairing the bridge required fishing the concrete decks out of the river channel with a crane and then carefully resetting them on the abutments. The first concern was if the concrete decks had been damaged when they were dropped into the river channel. The second concern was if big enough equipment would be available to lift the big, heavy slabs. The third concern was how could the lifting mechanism be fastened onto slabs that were partially sunk. And finally, it was no small concern for being able to work safely over and in the flowing waters of the Bear River. Bob loved those challenges. I was sure not to let the Regional Office know that we were planning to work on that bridge anytime soon. I figured this was going to be a heck of a lot of fun.

Bob went right to work by contacting Bill Dolling, a structural engineer he knew from his days at Thiokol. Bob had Bill come out and take a look at the condition of the slabs, then go back and calculate whether or not the slabs were still structurally sound enough to function safely if they were to be reset on the abutments. Bill finished his analysis overnight (I told you they did not waste any time) and reported the slabs were still strong enough to do the job. Great! Bob was on to figuring out what equipment he would need. After calculating the weight of each slab, Bob went looking for a crane and operator sufficient to do the job. He found the right crane and operator in the Logan area. But money was going to be a problem. Cranes are expensive and operators are paid top dollar. Once again, Bob "put the touch" on the owner and somehow negotiated a deal for $4,000 to reset all the slabs. That money included mobilization to the Refuge. Bob could negotiate great deals because he was setting the example by giving his own time and resources to the Refuge cause.

It was decided to use a strap to cradle the sunken decks and lift them into place. Bob reckoned he could launch his fishing boat and tie off on each abutment, then use a pole to feed the strap under the slab- - even though there was a flowing current. A day prior to the arrival of the crane, I had to leave on scheduled law enforcement training in Marana, Arizona for a week. Bummer for me. No, that would be a double bummer because I really wanted to see this process. At my training facility, I only had access to a couple of outside pay phones. So after a couple of days, I called Bob to get a status. He declared, "We are all done with the bridge decks Boss." I was impressed, thrilled and proud all at the same time. Immediately, I called Barney and said the volunteers had successfully rebuilt the main bridge. Barney could hardly believe it and I have to give him a lot of credit for not playing the administrator's role of asking about approvals from Safety, Engineering, etc. We just had a small celebration together over the phone. Man was I stoked and couldn't wait to get home and see what was going to happen next.

Bob's roster of volunteers was growing and would soon hit 50 people he could call on for various jobs. The next major hurdle was replacing the catwalks, guardrails and stoplogs on the major bridges and water control structures throughout the Refuge. This required use of several privately owned pickups and power tools. It also required a great deal of dimensional lumber to be cut and spliced into "flashboards," six foot long boards that are slid into concrete grooves to hold water flows water back and fill marshes. The hundreds of original flashboards were all removed during the flood and eventually carried away by the shifting floodwaters of Great Salt Lake. Now, the volunteers had to transport load after load out to each location and reinstall them. But first, catwalks had to be replaced because the floodwaters had ripped them from each structure. To complete the rehab of water control structures, new guardrails were also needed. That required a lot of steel posts, decking and some kind of railing system. Working with that much steel would require some special tools, materials and skill. Bob went to work solving that problem without skipping stride.

His solution was to engage the good will of a local steel production facility -Nucor Steel. They agreed to supply the materials and even send an employee to the Refuge to work with the volunteers at no cost. They designed a system of steel posts made from heavy angle iron with a railing that consisted of steel cable strung through the posts and pulled tight. It wasn't pretty, but it was functional. This was another design that I did not ask to be approved through the Regional Office. We just installed them and went on our merry way.

I was out giving the volunteers a hand one day when they were cleaning up around the Refuge entrance. The historic Refuge entrance sign had been an icon for decades. It was a large redwood sign with routed letters and was graced with the large image of a flying tundra swan. It sat atop a stonework base which gave the sign a timeless, rustic character. It was photographed innumerable times by visitors over the decades.

As floodwaters receded, the sign was nowhere to be seen and the base was pushed from its original location into the river channel. While being "bulldozed" by ice, it had also been turned upside down. So there it was, an upside down base half buried in mud on the edge of the river channel. Ugly I thought and not worth a second of our time to rehab. Bob thought different. He fired up the dozer and backed up to the river. I received his orders to wade in and hook up the chain so he could pull that concrete behemoth back to its original location on dry land (several hundred feet). I obeyed Bob's *orders* and then backed away as the dozer's treads dug into the bare ground and put a strain on the chain. Luckily, the chain held and the dozer snaked that oversized rock out of the river. With a little tugging and pushing, Bob got the foundation of the base just where he wanted it--level and ready to receive a new sign.

While fumbling around the riverbank with the chain, I hit a wooden plank with my foot. I pulled it out of the mud and discovered it was one of the redwood planks of the original sign. It was in bad shape from six years of salt water, mud and the elements. I figured it would make a good fire, so I started pulling other planks out of the mud and launching them underhand onto a pile (no, I was not going to get a burning permit from the Service's Fire Management Office). Then I heard Bob's *corrective* tone of voice yelling at me. In no uncertain terms he instructed me to show that sign some respect because he had a volunteer who was a professional sign painter and they were going to rehab the sign. "What," I said to myself. "This pile of scrap lumber is only good for starting a fire and has no chance of being made into a sign." But orders are orders, so I swallowed my pride and neatly stacked the planks into Bob's pickup.

Those planks were delivered to Jack Bradford's house and over the next few weeks he reassembled them on a plywood backing so they could be stabilized and scrubbed clean. Finally, he re-routed the letters and swan image. He completed the job with several coats of stain and filled the routed letters with white epoxy to match the original. The swan image was carefully repainted. Bob mounted the sign back on the original foundation and "Viola," the Refuge had a resurrected image from its past and one that all the locals recognized. Somehow, it brought back a small glimmer of the past glory.

During the spring and summer of 1990, my 7th grade son Ryan was getting his debut as the youngest volunteer. Yes, I know he was under 18 (14 to be exact) and not supposed to run equipment, drive or do much of anything except really safe (boring) stuff with basic hand tools like shovels. Instead, he had the summer of his life under Bob's "wing." Among other things, the Refuge was a great place to learn to drive a pickup, run power tools and hang out all day long with grandfather era men. One day, during the cleanup phase of work at the old headquarters site, Bob decided it was time to pull the old tower out of the marsh. This 100 foot steel framed tower was knocked down by ice flows and now lay buried under water and partially sunk in mud. Since Ryan was the most agile volunteer, he got the assignment to swim/wade/dive with a tow chain and hook it up to the end of the tower. After several tries (I was told), Ryan successfully pulled the chain to where it needed to be, then dove underwater to hook it on. With the muscle of Bob's four wheel drive pickup, the tower was coaxed out of the marsh and back up on dry land where it was hauled off as scrap. I never worried about Ryan's safety: the well-seasoned senior volunteers adored him and treated him like one of their own. He learned a lot about work and life that summer--maybe too much! He helped with a variety of tasks, including surveying while under the direction of volunteer Quinn Eskelsen. Together, they surveyed the dike elevations to help determine how much the dikes had eroded from the floodwaters.

Bob's growing roster of volunteers included folks with a broad variety of skills. We had everything from mechanics, surveyors and contractors. There was a volunteer for just about any skill required.

As spring runoff began, the volunteers had the water control structures in condition to begin impounding fresh water. The lowest breeches in "D" line, the main perimeter dike, had been repaired and otherwise the dikes were ok for impounding at least some water. Fresh water was diverted into all 5 units and the volunteers were anxious, along with me, to see if alkali bulrush would return. In early 1990, the landscape was completely barren for miles. Everyone was wondering how long it would take for the marshes to begin growing vegetation again.

Not long after that, I was walking with Bob Ebeling on the dike around unit 1A and spotted a small shoot of vegetation barley peeking above the dry, crusted mudflat. I got on my knees and dug the plant up with my pocket knife. Sure enough, it was a stalk of alkali bulrush sprouting from a tuber. It was cause for excitement because that tuber had survived 5 years of being submerged in briny water: now it was responding to a minimal flow of fresh water by sending up a single green shoot. I shouted that news to everyone I knew. It meant the marshes would bounce back quicker than most of us were expecting. Some fellow professionals even suggested I write up the discovery for publication, since it seemed so unlikely.

Fundraising was a major issue since no funding for construction had been budgeted by the Fish and Wildlife Service. Besides Bob's

donations of money, materials and vehicles, a serious level of donations were needed to keep the work moving forward without delay.
Discounts on heavy equipment use (Whitaker Construction) and
steel products (NuCor) helped, but cold hard cash was still needed.
Accomplishing on-the-ground projects required operating out of the
exact opposite side of the brain! I wondered how Bob would be able to
shift gears into the realm of asking for dollars.

Our very first donation came by surprise from the Bear River
Club before either Bob or I made a request. The club president Frosty
Braden announced a gift of $3,000 to help with the volunteers. That
was one thing (as impressive as it was), but fundraising would require
funding a total Refuge overhaul. "WOW, that was easy," I thought. It
wasn't huge, but it was a start and I was glad to get it. Next, Ducks
Unlimited came through with $10,000 after Bob put some pressure
on their local coordinator. I should say Bob put a lot of pressure on
them until they realized he was not going away! We got some good
press on that donation. Next came a donation from Browning, then the
Utah Wetlands Foundation and the Pintail Club. It seemed as though
donating to the volunteer restoration effort was an *in thing.* When it
was tallied up, the volunteers received $50,000 in cash and $15,000
worth of "in kind" donations in 1990. Since none of the volunteers
could actually accept the money, the Box Elder Wildlife Federation
set up an account in the name of "Friends of the Refuge." They had
a non-profit status for tax purposes and could handle the money for
the volunteers. It was a simple matter of Bob just calling the treasurer
and having a check written to whomever he wanted for supplies or
services. I did not bother asking the proper Fish and Wildlife Service
financial administrators if our accounting process was in compliance
with government policy. We just went ahead.

That first year, I was completely in the dark about the daily nuts-
and-bolts of water management. With dozens of water diversions in

operation it was necessary to adjust each of them as daily water inflows from the Bear River changed. The impoundments needed to be held to the right depth and the excess flows needed to be passed through the Refuge into Great Salt Lake. Bob knew all about that process because he was a hydrologic engineer by trade and had also taken a personal interest in the Refuge for over 20 years. He trained enough volunteers to help him make the rounds on a scheduled basis to keep the water flowing correctly. I assisted, but the job was way too big for any one person.

Utah State University Professor John Kadlec gave me a call one Spring day and introduced himself. He expressed an interest in the Refuge and told me about some of the studies he helped with on the marshes. I appreciated the call, but I had worked from time to time with college professors and frankly I was not overly impressed. They were ok, don't get me wrong, but they really were not all that much help either. I thought they lived in a world of research and information, but had little experience in management with real world issues. I also thought they tended to be on the arrogant side. I normally took their advice but had to temper it with reality before using it. As it would turn out, my stereotype far underestimated John's intellect and practical advice. And truth be known, I was also far overestimating my own intellect and abilities! John specialized in marsh management; he really knew his stuff.

John invited me up the USU campus and he offered to help out with the restoration. He had approval to spend a segment of his time on issues related to refuge redevelopment. I invited him to the Refuge for a day and we soon developed a close working relationship. I knew he was "for real" when I fired some questions to him and I received accurate and usable advice. He would become an important part of my trusted consultants for the rest of my career. More about John later.

As June of 1990 arrived, it was evident that the volunteers were going to meet their goal of opening the Refuge to the public by July 4! We were all stoked. Volunteers were somewhere on the Refuge 7 days a week. The volunteers opted for a ribbon cutting ceremony at the entrance of the tour route. The landscape was still barren and the old headquarters site was cleaned up, but by no means a pleasant sight. We borrowed a flatbed trailer full of folding chairs from our church and also a podium for the speakers. Once the chairs were set up, the flatbed was pulled in front and the podium set on top. Presto, we were set for the celebration once the ribbon was stretched across the road. To help with the celebration, Maddox restaurant brought out fried chicken with all the trimmings at no cost. Speakers included Congressman Jim Hansen, County Commissioner Bob Valentine and George Ward, president of the Box Elder Wildlife Federation. The event was covered by the Ogden Standard Examiner, Box Elder News Journal and television stations from Salt Lake City. I had a hard time soaking up all the support from top to bottom. In the earlier days of my career in the Dakotas and Nebraska I could not have dreamed of a refuge having this much support.

The ribbon was cut and cars made their way around the 13 mile tour route for the first time since 1984, with Bob Ebeling leading the way. It was a day like none other for me. It marked the successful goal of an all volunteer effort. All doubt was removed from my mind that things would come together for Bear River Migratory Bird Refuge and it would be rebuilt into something greater than before.

CHAPTER 9

"LET ME KNOW IF YOU NEED SOME HELP," OR HOW TO BUMBLE INTO A GOOD THING

Late in the fall of 1989, I was attempting to meet all the main local players including the Mayor of Brigham City and the three Box Elder County Commissioners. It was the end of a long day and I had one commissioner left to meet. The first two commissioners seemed friendly enough and I was hopeful that we could develop a good working relationship. I carried ugly memories of the County Commissioners in Nebraska, North Dakota and South Dakota. It was a struggle to work with them; they just didn't like the Fish and Wildlife Service. It could have been because we represented the Federal Government and we were invading their turf.

So on over I went to meet the last commissioner, Bob Valentine. I came to his office door and gave a knock. The conversation that followed was going to mark another career milestone every bit as big as meeting Bob Ebeling. In retrospect, it was amazing how I just bumbled into career-changing events without realizing it at the time.

I think it was God's hand "opening doors" for me that I was not even aware of. This was to be the first day of a lasting friendship. As the years unfolded, Bob would prove himself to be an unwavering supporter of the Refuge and the kind of guy who gave freely of his time, talents and influence. He asked nothing in return.

I soon discovered that Bob was an avid conservationist. He was involved with Ducks Unlimited, Utah Wetlands Foundation as well as the Utah Division Of Wildlife. Bob was also a serious waterfowl hunter and he even developed the Davis Duck Club. He had spent decades giving his time and financial donations to a broad variety of conservation organizations. He was even politically connected to the Governor as well as Senators Hatch and Bennett. And even better, he was personal friends with Congressman Jim Hansen. Wow, I thought to myself, I had never met a County Commissioner so friendly to conservation and well connected.

During our conversation, Bob let me know he was in favor of the Refuge and helping it get restored. Then he made a statement that would be pivotal to both my career and the restoration of the Refuge. Bob simply said, "Let me know if you need some help." Little did I know how much help he would give over the next 25 years and how important he would become to the restoration of the Refuge. Once again I was just clueless as to how much I had just been offered. Kind of like my clueless meeting of Bob Ebeling. Guess that shows how dense I was!

I was just loving the prospect that a real-life county commissioner was actually on my side, so I began to frequent Bob's office. In the spring of 1990, Bob asked me if we could use some special funding. "What??," I thought, "are you kidding?" I had no idea what he meant by "special funding," but one thing was for sure: the Federal budgeting cycle for 1990 was over and funds for individual refuges had long since been allocated. This was way, way too late to do anything for the current year. In fact, budgets for fiscal year 1991 were now in the "mill." Besides, I thought, Bob has no idea how tight funding is within the Division of Refuges. I had no problem with him trying for his so-called special funds, but I knew he was going to fail and at the same time get educated on how difficult it is to pry money out of Washington for your hometown refuge. Bob said something about calling his friend John Turner, who just happened to be the current director of the Fish and Wildlife Service.

I reacted by thinking, "Ok, sure, whatever, good luck." "Hope you don't get discouraged." Did I mention Bob also said something about asking for $75,000? This may not sound like much if you are from a big agency, but most of us refuge managers thought anything over $5,000 was worth fighting for. We came up through the ranks on shoestring budgets and were used to just barely getting along. I was so pleased that Bob would at least try, his support was encouraging even if came up empty handed.

I did not bother to say anything to my Regional Supervisor Barney Schranck because I really didn't think the request would go anywhere. Heck, I didn't even think he would get a conversation with Turner, let alone consideration for $75,000. However, a few weeks went by and I got a call from Barney. He was puzzled over a communication from Washington stating that a special appropriation had been earmarked by John Turner for Bear River Migratory Bird Refuge. It was $75,000 and it came from a pot of money called "The Directors Fund." Are you kidding me? Really, come on, ARE YOU KIDDING ME? I told Barney about Bob's previous offer to call director Turner for money. That was the beginning of my education into how a well connected citizen could open doors that are shut tight to the average government employee like me. I *never* doubted Bob again when he said he could do something.

We got right to task and awarded contracts to patch up the radial gates at headquarters, remove silt from the Whistler Canal and add dirt to the most damaged dike sections. This was exciting stuff--actually having a purse of money to get something done via private contractor.

Right after that, Bob made another offer. This time I took him seriously from the start. He recommended I put together a presentation for Congressman Jim Hansen about the Refuge and our needs. Bob said he could get Hansen to Brigham City for a one-on-one meeting with me. WOW, YIKES, REALLY? By now I was aware enough to realize that this could prove to be another pivotal point for both me and the Refuge. I was stoked and also really scared about messing things up.

More specifics about the meeting later on, but suffice it to say it was the beginning of a three-way team. Looking back, that "partnership" was also a career highlight.

By now it was clear to me that I was not engineering all the good stuff that was happening all around me. A lot of it was being dumped in my lap. Do you believe in a God who helps average "Joes" do things they cannot accomplish on their own? Well, I do. This was just the beginning.

Bob Valentine became a very successful person with political clout and a large (very large) network of dedicated friends due to his strong character. Decades later, I asked him what he thought the "magic ingredient was" for his accomplishments. He explained that it was simple: Never lie to someone, don't create enemies, never take more than you need from a negotiation and always give respect to others. I saw him hold to those qualities many times over the years. He never became angry and never put people down. He was able to maintain communication with all the players, no matter how contentious the issue became. And believe me, it got contentious with some

Regional Office staff later on when it seemed we were circumventing their authority. Bob was the kind of guy who would not interrupt someone during a discussion. At the same time, he would stop speaking even if he was the one being rudely interrupted. It was a matter of showing respect even when the other person did not always deserve it. He did his best to find a win-win for everyone with a vested interest. He once corrected me when I commented that he had gained power through his personal attributes. Bob said he never wanted nor sought power, he only hoped to be effective.

That is the brief profile of a man that I would soon come to rely on for virtually every hot issue I had to tackle at the Refuge.

CHAPTER 10

THE WAY FORWARD-THE NEED TO REDESIGN

It was not a viable option to rebuild the Refuge back exactly the way it was before the flood. Some basic flaws in design and operation were coming to light over the decades from the 1940's to the early 1980's when the flood hit. As biological data was analyzed from the Refuge files, some negative trends became obvious.

Botulism, a bacterial disease, was steadily increasing over the decades. Even though the Refuge was established to slow the spread of Botulism, somehow the Refuge was not solving the problem. It was slowly getting worse. Waterfowl production was also declining over the years. Bear River had once been considered a prime area for nesting waterfowl. However, nest surveys over the final decades were showing a long decline. Legal waterfowl harvest by hunters was likewise on a slow decline. So, what was going on?

A team of biologists was brought in during the late 1970's. Their conclusion was that overall biological productivity was declining because the design and operation of the Refuge had been too stable for too long. In English that means the 5 large impoundments had been filled with water and held at the same depth for too many years in a row. The wetland units were filled with water each spring to a specified depth and then held there till late fall and then lowered to a winter depth. That cycle was repeated every year. Since the 5 units were huge (5,000 acres each), they were difficult to manage. Changes in water levels meant that huge amounts of water had to be dumped out of the Refuge to lower a unit. Then refilling was impossible because river flows were not high enough a good part of the year. So, the big units did not lend themselves to intentionally planned fluctuations for management purposes.

The original design also operated by diverting river water into the top portion of each unit. All 1.2 million acre/feet of annual Bear River water flows had to be run into the 5 units and through the perimeter dike. That caused the overall salinity of the impoundments to become fresher than optimum, a problem not foreseen in 1928. The large units varied in depth from inches in the shallows at the upper end to several feet in the deep areas near the perimeter dike. Providing a consistent wetland depth was impossible.

Carp populations were also a negative impact. With untold thousands living in the Bear River channel, carp had an open door to access the Refuge marshes. These "marsh hogs" grew to gigantic size and degraded the marsh by destroying vegetation and creating muddy water so desirable vegetation could not grow. The original Refuge had a "borrow pit" running parallel to the dikes. These pits, several feet deep, is where dirt was taken by steam shovels to construct the dike. These canals were perfect deep water zones for carp to survive during the extremes of summer or winter. They could not be intentionally drained by managers to rid the marsh of carp. Another design improvement needed was a series of bypass canals that would allow managers to divert high spring flows around impounded units rather than through them. This was important because birds would nest by the thousands each spring in the marsh. Then higher river flows would arrive in June when snowmelt reached a peak in the mountains. There was no way to prevent this surge of water from flooding nests. Bypass canals would provide a means to divert those excess flows around important nesting units and directly into Great Salt Lake where they are normally welcomed.

All those design recommendations may seem like the biological team was beating up on Van Wilson, the author of the original design. Please. It is not that way. Van took a degraded area of 100 square miles in 1928 and made it into the model of wildlife conservation for a generation of scientists as well as the general public. The field of Wildlife Management was advanced greatly by his efforts. However, lessons were to be learned and improvements were to be recommended. That process is at the heart of a process called "adaptive management."

And a little secret here--promise not to tell anyone? The improvements we made in this round will not all be perfect either. Bummer.....

Another deficiency was evident. The Refuge had very little upland habitat. It was made up primarily of marshes. Grassland nesting birds had little area to do their thing. So, it was noted that the addition of surrounding uplands would be valuable for protecting a variety of species into the future. It was assumed that land development would hit this area of the Wasatch front in the coming decades, driving the necessity of acquiring areas surrounding the Refuge that are currently in private farming/ranching operations. More Federal land acquisition in a state that is already a majority of Federal lands? That should go over big with the Box Elder County Commission and Governor....

And last, but not least, was the issue of replacing the headquarters buildings. These included a visitor center, office, maintenance buildings, residences and campground. Since the site was now under the 100 year flood zone for sure, an alternate site would have to be identified and purchased. Then a whole new headquarters complex would need to be designed and, somehow, funded.

So, there it was-- a big barren mudflat that could not be restored back to what it used to be. But what would the future plan be and how would the new concept look when it was all put together on paper? With no guidance and commitment from Washington or the Regional Office, how could this all come together? Who would do what? I had more questions than answers, and I was the Refuge Manager *for crying out loud*!

How and where to begin making a way forward in all that chaos? Well, enter Harvey Whitmier, a land acquisition specialist in the Regional Office. He had organizational skills and also good common sense. I listened to his advice just because it was usually helpful. Harvey was also a good listener; that helped a lot. It was Harvey that came up with the solution. The Refuge would be restored as a three-step plan, with the underlying principle *Wildlife First*, meaning public use and all other developments would be done only after our basic wildlife mission was accomplished. Here is how it panned out:

Step 1 -Restore the historic (old) water management system and operate it as best we could.

Step 2 -Enhance the water management system via a new design with smaller units, new bypass canals and more water control structures. This step would address all of the issues presented by the biological team in the late 1970's. Further, expand the Refuge by thousands of acres to encompass high quality grasslands for nesting, and at the same time purchase easements on privately owned wetlands to protect them in perpetuity.

Step 3 -Design and build a new headquarters complex, including an education center on some of the newly purchased lands near the Interstate 15 exit at Forest Street.

So we had a plan, but it did not obligate any funds to make it happen. It did not even nail down significant agency support at the Washington level where budgets are formulated. We had a plan that the Friends bought into and my supervisor Barney Schranck supported, but it didn't go much beyond that. We were pretty much on our own with a nice plan on paper. But hey, I later found out that a plan on paper is important as you make appeals for money from various sources.

One more important element of the plan, it was conceived and developed with the full input from the group of volunteers who would eventually incorporate into an official "Friends of Bear River Migratory Bird Refuge" organization (more on that later). They just called themselves *The Friends*. There was buy- in from the start and we developed the vision together. As we talked about a new Visitor Center and developed *our* vision, it was agreed that we should go for something that would be on par with the best in the nation. That sounds naive, but as I found out later they were dead serious. Years later, when the time had come for initiating the design work and funding sources, key individuals within the Friends organization made it happen. I will pick up on that story a bit later.

At that time, I was completely dumb about what it took to plan, design and build a Visitor Center. I knew nothing about the agency construction process or the details to be considered when designing a public use facility for the general public. I would have been overwhelmed at that point if I would have known what I did not know.

All I could think was "alrighty then, lets go ahead and build the best Visitor Center in the nation." I am sure glad God loves fools. I was in for a real education and also for the time of my life.

CHAPTER 11

CONGRESSMAN JAMES V. HANSEN

Once the corps of volunteers began the restoration process, Congressman Hansen proved to be a critical long term link to the restoration. He provided our inside track to Washington D.C. that would eventually bring a flow of earmarked funds for the restoration. Funds allocated by Washington for specific use in a designated site are termed "earmarked." Agency administrators don't like receiving earmarked funds because they have no authority to redirect that money to other pet projects they may have. Those dollars must be spent where, and only where, Congress intended. I loved earmarked funding, but it irked some folks in my agency and that was ok with me. Earmarks are uncommon because most refuge managers just don't get a chance to play in the Washington D.C. arena. The upper level agency personnel liked to handle everything at that level. Congressman Hansen's direct ties with Bear River Migratory Bird Refuge were a rare opportunity and I did not take it for granted at all.

Upon arrival in Brigham City, I had no clue as to the scope or cost of what lay ahead. In the first months I became familiar with the current state of events. Everything, and I mean everything, was broken or destroyed. With Bob Ebeling coming on board, I used him as my official assistant (although he was unofficial in the eyes of the government). His 30 year history with the Refuge was an invaluable treasure trove of knowledge. And Bob was not shy about sharing his knowledge or opinion about how things use to be and how things should be fixed and improved. By spring of 1990, I began to have a good feel of the size and scope of what we were facing. Volunteers under Bob's supervision were on the Refuge daily. His cadre of personnel was approaching 50 dedicated souls. The restoration projects were running on donated materials, services and funds and the days were full of excitement. By this time I was getting a good feel of what it would take to complete the massive job ahead of us. I was unsettled about how we would acquire the funding needed in the long run, even though the volunteers were moving along quite well in the present. Still, I was nagged by the reality that we had nobody in the upper levels of the U.S. Fish and Wildlife Service organization who were supporting our future.

Then, with one offer by Bob Valentine, our future was about to take a turn for the better. "I'll get Jim Hansen down here for a Refuge tour," Bob offered. "You can show him what is going on and get him on board with the restoration," he further explained. We planned out a day with the Congressman that included a slide show of the past, present and future needs. Following, we intended to do a "show me" tour of the Refuge complete with observing the work being done by the volunteers. At that time we routinely had 30 to 50 volunteers working daily on the Refuge. It was impressive and exciting. I knew if Congressman Hansen could be out with the volunteers for even a short visit, he would be inspired by their dedication.

When I was planning the Refuge tour and slide show for Congressman Hansen, I knew I was over my head. Doing Refuge work was one thing, but actually cultivating a relationship with a member of Congress was a whole other ball game. I was scared and overwhelmed to think I was going to be the main agency contact with the Congressman for a day. I would come to discover that spending time with Congressmen and Senators was a good thing, but back then it was unknown territory for me. It just seemed that Regional Staff would magically do a better job than I could.

When we met for the first time on the morning of the tour, Bob Valentine broke the ice and got us started in what would become a very rewarding relationship over the next 16 years. When we finished the slide show and completed the tour, Congressman Hansen pulled Bob Valentine and me aside to say he would support the restoration of the Refuge.

Wow! Think of that: one day we had no prospects of long term funding for restoration and in a single day we had a Congressman promising us help. I was elated because Bob Valentine had done a huge favor for the Refuge and he was my local contact whom I could see in person anytime. It just does not get any better than that for a refuge manager. This added up to be another promise that Bob Valentine made and kept. I was soon to realize that his word was solid. Over the next decade he would keep every promise he made from Brigham City to Washington D.C.

And as for Jim Hansen, he would champion the Refuge in Washington without fail from the first earthmoving contracts to the final construction of the Education Center. The Refuge team now consisted of the volunteers, Bob Valentine and Jim Hansen. I was loving this new aspect of my job.

CHAPTER 12

OTHERS JOIN THE TEAM; WELCOME ABOARD

Right before my move to Brigham City, the regional office arranged for a rented space to serve as my office upon my arrival in August of 1989. It was supposed to be adequate for my needs and I guess it was, but I hated being inside it. This so-called office consisted of two small, drab windowless rooms about the size of an average bedroom. If that were not dreary enough, the entry door was solid wood, so when it was shut, the office walls really closed in on me. Being without communication (no computer and before cell phone days), I went down to the local Fred Meyer store and bought a telephone. I could call out, but very few people had my new number. It was rare to get an incoming call in those early days, so I was delighted to get a call one day from a professor at Utah State University. "My name is John Kadlec, professor in the Wildlife Biology Department," the caller stated. After a short introduction John invited me to campus in Logan for a meeting over lunch. That meeting was to be another fortuitous event for the future of the Refuge.

As it turned out, John was a professor held in high regard by other faculty and students as well. His expertise was in wetland management and he was experienced specifically with the salt marshes in this area. He had conducted studies in Northern Utah since the 1970's and was also familiar with the historic literature. Privately owned hunt clubs had contracted with Professor Kadlec to design their water management systems, so his skill was known even among private organizations. This guy, I soon discovered, was a treasure trove of knowledge and held valuable insight into what needed to be done to improve Refuge water management programs.

Unfortunately, my career up to this point had interfaced with professors who were generally not that helpful in the realm of management. I had developed over time a rather dim view of how much on-the- ground advice I could use from "academia." Professor Kadlec was about to crush my stereotype and show me what kind of help a sharp professor could provide. I just had to get rid of some personal pride and open my ears. John offered a substantial amount of time from his schedule to help with the Refuge restoration. It would cost me nothing. All he needed was my approval for him to join the Refuge team and offer whatever skills he had. After our first meeting, I had a good feeling about John's credentials as well as his interpersonal skills, so I agreed. Since it was free, I really was not taking much of a risk. I thought I could just ignore whatever advice I did not think was helpful.

As happened so many times, I grossly *underestimated* what he would eventually contribute to our efforts. This is another point in the restoration story where it seems God was sending someone especially suited to do a special job at just the right time.

John began visiting the Refuge on a regular basis and we became very good friends. Soon, he gained my confidence as a first rate consultant. His advice was not only academically correct, it was practical! As the restoration progressed, John's advice was used throughout the design process and subsequent management programs. He was especially helpful in designing the new water management system which included inlet and bypass canals. He also played a major role in long range water management planning and botulism control strategies. When the "Friends of the Refuge" were officially organized as an official support organization for the Refuge, he joined the Board of Directors and remained active until shortly before his death. His final contribution was to help secure private funds for the Education Center. Chapter 29 describes more about his successful fundraising.

In the fall of 1989, Bob Ebeling was able to make some initial progress before winter hit. He recruited a retired contractor, Wayne Jensen, to help him plan construction activities. Coming on board as well was Jerry Mason, the General Manager (retired) of Thiokol and Bob's previous supervisor at work. Jerry was in charge and gave the final go-ahead for the disastrous launch of the Challenger space shuttle. Bob had strongly opposed the launch, but was overridden by Jerry. Needless to say, their relationship after that was strained. But, their work at the Refuge brought them together on neutral ground for the common goal of Refuge restoration. In addition, Jerry's role was more political and behind the scenes, while Bob was hands on. By December of 1989, the stage was set for an influx of help from various sources. Bob indicated to the public that volunteers would reopen the Refuge to public use by July 4, 1990 even though the U.S. Fish and Wildlife Service had not yet officially decided to restore the Refuge at all. By December of 1989, Ebeling was hard at work lining up his plan-of-attack for securing the labor and materials he would need as soon as winter would break. Whatever he planned, it would have to be done efficiently to meet his July 4 deadline.

Bob "put the touch," as he called it, on numerous groups and individuals for donations. I had never seen anything like what was happening. The Brigham City Council asked me to give a presentation at a regular meeting. I was surprised by a round of applause at the conclusion. Then one city councilman pulled his checkbook out and give me a personal check right up front! This was really getting to be fun. Totaled up, the cash gifts were $13,000 by the end of December. That may not sound like much (remember those were 1989 dollars), but Bob made every dollar stretch by always negotiating for reduced prices. After a little practice, he became skilled at soliciting. I can say with confidence that the vast majority of purchases were made at, or below, cost from the supplier. And hey, this whole idea of raising money from private donations to run a refuge was new to all of us. We were all inexperienced at the get-go.

When 1990 arrived the lid was blown off anything that resembled status quo. Our donor list increased to 41 total. All since the fall of 1989! Likewise, the corps of volunteers exceeded 50 individuals, most from our Brigham City community. Being the sole "government man" among a sea of volunteers who were being funded by non-government sources, I was unfettered by *agency judgment*. In other words, the volunteers did things the most expedient way and we cast red tape to the wind. I knew we (or more correctly "I") were technically doing a lot of things illegally since we were not going through any channels for approval to do what we were doing. I simply reported work done after it was finished. Fun, Fun Fun! In my little pea brain I concluded that as long as we were doing the job cheaper and better, how could anyone in the government fault us??

A corps of around 50 volunteers joined the Refuge effort that spring and summer. Exact numbers are unrecorded. I just thought it was more important to focus on getting projects done than document- ing every volunteer who helped. I estimate 50 volunteers, and I have no total of what hours they contributed in 1990.

In early 1990, the regional office in Denver recognized I was in need of additional paid staff. One position was critically necessary because an "Environmental Assessment" had to be written before an official decision could be made to either restore, enhance, expand or divest of the Refuge. This document would take one full time staff person nearly two years to complete. The second position approved was for an Administrative Assistant (clerk-secretary) to handle the office paperwork. These positions were filled in January, much to my delight. Both new employees, Cherry Fisher and Keith Hansen were exceptional. They caught the volunteer vision and added to the momentum extensively. Late in 1990, I was allowed to hire an assistant (also called a deputy). Claire Caldes transferred in to fill that position and wound up staying about 10 years. So, by the end of 1990 three permanent full time staff had arrived to join the corps of 50 volunteers. These were exciting times. Our local people were leading the effort, not a far-- off government agency.

CHAPTER 13

DAM THE RIVER, FULL SPEED AHEAD

From the very beginning of the restoration, an issue boiled at the state capital in Salt Lake City. It seems that during the flood years (1983-1988), state officials were trying to figure out how to deal with too much water in the Bear River and subsequently raising Great Salt Lake to flood levels. Millions were appropriated for the Utah Department of Water Resources to evaluate how a series of dams on the Bear River could withhold enough water to reduce flooding of Great Salt Lake, and a "Bear River Task Force" was organized to oversee the effort.

They zeroed in on the Bear River because it alone contributes 60% of the total inflow to Great Salt Lake. After spending a lot of time and money, the conclusion was NO. That is, not even a whole series of dams on the Bear River could hold enough water back if the 1983-1987 flood conditions returned. So it would seem the answer was provided and now everyone could go home and live happily ever after.

But not so fast! Even though dams could not effectively reduce major flooding, why not keep the same task force going to evaluate an opposite question. Here goes. Where can dams be built to provide a water supply for future municipal and industrial developments? Well, yea. Now we can keep meeting monthly, appropriate more money for water development planning and hopefully (cross your fingers here), build a brand new dam somewhere on the Bear River.

We did not dare turn our backs on this exercise, so we spent a day of my time every month sitting in Task Force meetings in the Capitol Building. And you guessed it, after a ton of torturous meetings, two sites were recommended for reservoirs and both were highly detrimental to the environment and wildlife. That led both the Fish and Wildlife Service as well as the Audubon Society to oppose the projects.

At a time when public support was so high for the Refuge, I hated being drawn into this controversial issue. Some of the State agency officials were attempting to paint the Refuge as a dangerous obstacle blocking potential water development for Utah's future use. We referred to the group of pro- development officials and lawyers as "water buffaloes". They struck a certain degree of fear in me.

The constant boiling and churning of this issue over the years would take a considerable amount of my time and energy away from what I considered productive work with restoring the Refuge. Now I had to take time to ensure the Bear River and it's upstream environs had a secure future. I never really finished, and I don't think the battle will be over for decades, if ever. Chapter 18 on Water Rights has more information.

CHAPTER 14

THE JAMISON UNIT: A NEW MARSH WITH UNLIKELY FRIENDS

Being neighbors with a large hunting club was a new experience for me. Named "The Bear River Club," it contained around 13,000 acres primarily of marsh and was managed by Gordon Schaefer, a full-time employee. Gordon intensively managed water levels with a diversion canal taking water out of the Malad River. Naturally, I enjoyed a good professional relationship with the club, but I was reluctant to become too "chummy." After all, the club was in existence primarily to hunt and kill waterfowl. They seemed ok as neighbors, but I just wanted to keep a close eye on how they operated. With high dollars invested, the temptation to exceed bag limits and ignore other restrictions was there. We were friendly enough and I liked the fact that they maintained a large marsh with their own water right. The Bear River Club had a long relationship with the Refuge and they were among the first organizations to donate to the restoration.

Gordon requested I join him and a Bear River Club member on a tour of their newest habitat projects. I was all for that, so Gordon introduced me to Max Jamison. Once again, this introduction would mark the beginning of a long term friendship with Max that would be fruitful for the Refuge. The year was 1991 and the restoration was in full swing.

What made my job fun was that I got to see top-notch wildlife sanctuaries and get paid for it! In this case it took most of a day to get around their managed marshes, view the wildlife use and see how their dikes and water controls maintained their system. We covered all the high points of waterfowl management like nesting, migrations, natural food production, predator control and managed hunting. The tour that day, however had a purpose that I was about to find out.

Finishing up our inspection of the Club's property on the northwest side, we were brought to the Refuge boundary on the east side of Unit 1. A fence separated the Club from the Refuge. Standing on the Club's side, a low dike was impounding shallow water that sustained a beautiful marsh dotted with stands of alkali bulrush, a plant favored by waterfowl for both food and cover. The Refuge lands beyond this lush boundary were a stark contrast of bare, dry mudflats to the horizon.

Gordon and Max brought me here to make a point and offer a proposal. "Our property looked just like your mudflat over there," Gordon explained. "If you build a dike along the same contour as ours, those mudflats will become a productive marsh just like ours," he continued. I was convinced, but funds were going to be a killer. I had none. Max jumped in and said the Bear River Club would be willing to help out with contributions and so would he personally.

Imagine that, neighbors and friends wanting to help with a federal refuge. That was a new concept and I could hardly believe my ears. I was sold on the idea right away. For once, I didn't have to come up with the idea myself and then try to get it funded through normal government channels, which would take years. So off we went, in agreement to develop a new marsh in the NE corner of Unit 1 funded by a partnership of donors. I could hardly wait to get back to tell Bob Ebeling we had a new project that we could add to the restoration -- as if we didn't have enough on our plate already!

Bob took to the project immediately; it was right up his alley. The marsh would cover over 600 acres and require a dike 1.5 miles long with a water control "spill box" to regulate water depth and discharges of excess flows. A need of $50,000 was calculated to cover the dirt work and spill box construction. Since private donations from Max and the Club were made, we applied for matching funds from the Fish and Wildlife Foundation. It was a perfect fit since they were in business to encourage private participation in conservation projects.

Ebeling provided the engineering and design, then found the best deal for an earthmoving contract. He found a dragline operator, running a machine that should have been retired decades before. But he could move dirt cheaper than anyone else, especially in the soft ground conditions on the mudflats. Ebeling and the volunteers formed the spill box foundations and sidewalls then placed the concrete.

It was that simple. A new unit was built. The landscape responded immediately to the newly impounded water and a showcase marsh was created and thousands of birds used it. Man is that ever rewarding!

To honor Max, we decided to surprise him and his wife Kay with a commemorative plaque mounted on the concrete spillway. We held a tour with a group of people and when we got to the Jamison Unit, I gave a presentation ceremony. I thought Max had a funny look on his face for a guy that had just received some accolades. Max pulled me aside and said the ceremony "busted him" because he had not told his wife Kay anything about giving money to the project! It was a total surprise to her. I can only hope she forgave him quickly.

The Bear River Club went on to partner with the Refuge in other projects including research studies and environmental education program development.

CHAPTER 15

BUREAU OF RECLAMATION OR "WRECK THE NATION"

The 1950's and 60's were notorious years for large dam building projects around the country and with it the extensive loss of wildlife habitat. Prior to the passage of the National Environmental Policy Act of 1970, engineers working for various governmental agencies could plan grandiose projects without regard to environmental harm. It wasn't even a consideration. Post WWII prosperity and the political mindset to develop wherever possible led to devastating results on the nation's rivers, prairies and wild areas.

One agency was particularly guilty (at least in the mind of conservationists): the U.S. Bureau of Reclamation. They had designed and built a myriad of reservoirs, irrigation districts and other projects that resulted in channelization, loss of river habitats, drainage of small wetlands and so forth. Their political and economic power seemed unstoppable at one time.

I hacked my way through college at Colorado State University from fall quarter of 1967 through spring quarter of 1971. During those academic years, my favorite college professor, Eugene Decker, termed their agency The Bureau of "Wreck the Nation." Funny. I thought it fit perfectly and freely used the agency slur with great joy throughout my career.

Quite by surprise, another one of my long–held prejudices was about to be shattered in 1991 when the phone rang and a fellow from the Bureau of Reclamation was on the other end of the line. I probably rolled my eyes as he introduced himself as Lee Baxter from the Provo office. Lee explained he was given orders to call me because the Bureau of Reclamation and U.S. Fish and Wildlife had signed a Memorandum of Understanding at the Washington D.C. level that pledged the agencies would work together for the benefit of the environment whenever possible. HHHHMMMMMMMM...

I had heard something about the agreement, but I really didn't think much about it. A lot of good intentions come and go in the government and you waste time trying to implement all of them. I had blown off any thought of getting something from "the Bureau." It was just a bunch of political hot air as far as I could tell.

But when I got the call, I wondered if there might be something to it. Lee said he was authorized to come visit the Refuge and see if there was something they could help us with. I quit rolling my eyes and started to listen. Lee arrived for a scheduled tour and began to impress me immediately. He was a tall slender guy with a good sense of humor and he seemed to have a grasp of the magnitude of what we were trying to accomplish. I took a liking to Lee right away, and I think he liked me as well. After getting familiar with the Refuge, Lee recommended that their engineering department help with some designing on the water management system we would eventually build. Sounded good to me, but that was a bit intangible at that exact point in time.

Before long I got another call from Lee. This time he alerted me that a "drought relief" bill had been passed by Congress. It enabled agencies to apply for funds to accomplish projects that would lessen the affects of the current drought across the west. You might ask, "Didn't the Refuge get destroyed by flooding?" Yes, good point. HOWEVER, nobody cared by then if a big—time agency was going to bat with a request of money for the Refuge. They simply had the machismo to make it happen, unlike the anemic U.S. Fish and Wildlife Service.

I was all ears as Lee said he would do the paperwork requesting $500,000 for projects on the Refuge! WOW... That was super good news. Not only were they going to put their muscle behind this request, they were going to do all the paperwork! I loved appropriations for the Refuge and hated paperwork so this was another dream deal. It didn't take long for Lee to call back telling me we were approved and I had the $500K sitting in an account for the Refuge. To make it EVEN SWEETER, the money could be held over a multi-year budgeting cycle. That is a big deal because spending all the money wisely usually requires time to procure the best deals in sequence with the progression of work. This money would not disappear at midnight September 30 of that fiscal year, it would stay on the books and carry over to the next year. That is a HUGE deal because it is hard to go through all the red tape of engineering, contracting and other regulators in less than a year. I was not under a tight time frame to spend the money. I know, that sounds really strange, but it is absolutely true.

I was not accustomed to "huge" sums of money like that. I came from an era and region that dealt money out in hundreds or thousands. This was a big deal and it left a pit in my stomach about spending funds like that. It was sure nice to have Lee on my team; he was from a big-money agency and would help me handle being in the big time! At long last, I had become a fat cat. To make things even better, Lee was like another employee on my staff but the Bureau of Reclamation was paying his entire salary!

When we began design plans for an entirely new water management system, Lee suggested that Reclamation could help with the engineering specifications of whatever we proposed. The original Refuge had 5 main Units of about 5,000 acres each. Conceptually, a new design would incorporate many smaller units so water could be regulated to improve wetland habitats. Planning new canals and water control structures would be necessary. So yes, we needed engineers attending the planning sessions for the water management system layout.

Soon, we mapped out the new layout. With the help of professor John Kadlec, adjacent managers from Salt Creek and Ogden Waterfowl Management Areas, and other biologists, we mapped out an entirely new system. Now, the Refuge would have 100 miles of diking, 100 water control structures and over 30 separate management units. Lee gathered up the sketches made that day and returned to Provo for engineering analysis and specific designs. I received a professionally produced map with the location of all facilities. In addition, all canals, dikes and water control structures were designed to accommodate the diversion volumes needed to do the job biologists had identified. That was slick!

By then I was embarrassed at my previous stereotype of Reclamation. Their people were putting themselves into our restoration efforts and making a big difference.

Next, we took on cross diking Unit 3. We used the $500K to purchase some equipment and supplies for completing numerous miles of dike, canal and a water control structures. Some money was also spent to produce a video explaining the need for restoring the refuge because we knew Congress would need to be motivated at some point in the near future. Some dirt moving contracts were awarded to work alongside our own volunteers and employees moving dirt.

As the original $500K was drawing down, Congress passed a "Flood Relief" bill. Go figure. I guess someone, somewhere had high water. It wasn't us, but the broad brush of the bill covered our area, so Lee applied--and received-- another $326,000 in 1994. Much of this funding was used to design and install a water monitoring system that Reclamation had successfully incorporated into their irrigation systems across the West. It was intended to improve water use efficiency, especially during the critical summer months when inflows varied with intermittent storms. It was termed "robo marsh" for its ability to automatically regulate inlet canals and water depths. In the long run, the system was partially successful.

Over a 5 year period, The Bureau of Reclamation provided extremely valuable help with initiating the restoration. The personal involvement of Lee Baxter was both a professional and personal help. I came to trust his judgment and appreciate his good will, along with his agency.

Once again, a simple phone call turned out to be someone offering services at just the right time. It also made me a much humbler person. Another one of my simple and ignorant stereotypes was shattered.

Coincidence, or does God love Bear River Refuge?

CHAPTER 16

EXPANDNG THE
REFUGE BOUNDARY

In 1928, when Bear River Refuge was established, it encompassed 64,500 acres. That is slightly over 100 square miles and you might think that is more than adequate. I would tell people that it was an extremely large back yard. As restoration of the Refuge was considered, we took a close look at the boundaries even though they had served well for over 6 decades.

This vast landholding included about 99% wetland habitat. Picture thousands of acres of mudflats that may have been covered by several inches of water temporarily during the spring and possibly part of the fall. Also picture the river channel of the Bear River as it entered its delta and spread out into numerous smaller channels that eventually fanned out into marshes. Finally, with your mind's eye picture thousands of acres of lush marshes several feet deep with bulrush stands scattered to the horizon. There was nothing "wrong" with those wetland areas, it is just that no upland areas were included. This meant that grassland habitat for nesting birds of all kinds was completely lacking from the Refuge. That was not a major problem up until the 1990's because the grasslands neighboring the Refuge were owned by ranchers and farmers who used the land in ways that were favorable to wildlife. Birds went back and forth from the Refuge to private lands to find food, nesting areas and places to rest. There existed a harmony with nature.

Not to crash that beautiful cooperative arrangement, but when we looked to the future it was evident that the use of those private lands by wildlife was coming to an end. The reason? Utah's human population is growing at an explosive rate, engulfing landscapes with houses, roads and other developments. Box Elder County had been spared from this tidal wave of people so far, but it is not going to be long before the development mania engulfs the areas surrounding the Refuge.

The solution: Refuge boundaries need to include enough surrounding grasslands to sustain bird populations when human land development is completed. So, we assumed what the Refuge did not own would become urban someday. All we had to do was look south and see what was happening adjacent to the state managed waterfowl management areas at Farmington Bay and Ogden Bay.

Our first step of action was to include a "Refuge Expansion" proposal in our long term plans. The actual boundary lines of our proposed acquisition was spelled out on a map in the Environmental Assessment written by Keith Hansen and later approved by Regional Director Galen Buterbaugh. It specified an area to be outright purchased--on a willing seller basis. The Environmental Assessment also specified an area of mixed wetland and upland acreage to be protected with an easement. The easement was targeted to protect lands currently being managed as marshes by hunt clubs. Altogether, this proposal to expand the Refuge boundary encompassed 39,000 acres (17,000 to be purchased and 22,000 to be placed under wetland easement). That is no small acquisition request for a State that was already 80% Federally owned. Now with this proposal, all we wanted was a little more!

When we were successful in getting our land acquisition proposal approved by the regional director, it essentially bounced the ball back into our court. Now the hard part was about to begin. Before we could go forward, federal legislation required that the Governor of Utah approve the plan. Oh NO... If you haven't checked lately, Utah is home to the most conservative politicians in the nation. How was I supposed to talk the Governor into approving the 39,000 acre acquisition of private land? I would be lucky to leave such a meeting without a king-sized tongue lashing. That is assuming the Governor would even take the time to talk to me.

Surprise! By this time Bob Valentine had become an active supporter of the Refuge and I gave him a call to see if he would help. The resulting phone call would be another key turning point for the future of the Refuge. Explaining to Bob that I needed Governor Norm Bangertor's signature on our acquisition plan, he replied without hesitation, "When do you want to see him?" "Whenever you make the appointment," I replied and we hung up. A few minutes later I picked up the phone and Bob told me our meeting was set up. I was so relieved that Bob was going with me, or maybe I should say I was going with Bob.

Never before had I experienced the comfort of having a trusted friend leading the way into a high stakes meeting. Failure in this meeting would kill our land acquisition plans. Bob was not some kind of a paid lobbyist, he was just a genuine supporter of the Refuge helping with a cause he believed in. We were ushered into the Governor's office and the three of us sat at the end of a long, long table. "Bob, good to see you," said the Governor, then looking over at me he asked, "Who is this with you?" I was introduced and we talked hunting and fishing for a while. Then the governor asked what he could do for us. That is when I turned totally chicken, I thought to myself, "Things could go south now when we ask for permission to buy private land."

I felt myself slump a little bit in the leather chair. But in a split second, Bob took over by saying "We need your signature to buy some land for the Refuge." "Is this a good deal Bob?", the Governor asked, "and will it be open to hunting?" Bob assured the Governor it was a good deal and it would be partially opened for hunting after going through an evaluation process to ensure compatibility with refuge purposes. The Governor replied, "OK then, where do I sign?" and it was over that quickly. Hey, this was a BIG DEAL!! The Governor could have stopped our acquisition plans, but his signature allowed us to proceed at our own pace.

I could not wait to call Harvey Wittmier, my land acquisition contact in the Regional Office. He was shocked when I told him Governor's approval was a "done deal." What a great day for the Refuge. I was having a ball. This is what private citizen advocacy was supposed to be at its best, and Bob is the one who came to me, not vice versa. It was hard for me to wrap my head around how *easy* it was for Bob to accomplish something nobody else in my organization could. I was beginning to get an idea of how influential Bob was. I liked it. I liked it a lot.

We began the land purchase effort by hosting a meeting for all landowners. In order to limit the rumor mill, we opted to have one big meeting where everyone heard the same basic information of what we were trying to do. We didn't make any offers, just gave information and answered questions. Right after that, I met with every landowner privately to see what their level of interest was. I was trying to find one landowner willing to sell immediately, just to get the ball rolling. In rural areas, landowners pay close attention to what other neighbors do. It is a big advantage if a major landowner sells and has a good experience with the process.

My break came soon. I approached a very senior rancher with a large extended family. Winn Nichols had "run cattle" on an 1,100 acre parcel for decades. Now he saw it was in the family's interest to sell the entire parcel and divide the money. VIOLA! That fits our program perfectly. We pay cash on the barrel head and we pay fair appraisal value. No hanky-panky with trying for low ball offers, just a fair price for the entire parcel at one closing. We had a "closing party" in my office with our reality staff and all of Winn's relatives who were required to sign (as I recall that amounted to over a dozen people). As the family filed out of the office, Winn lingered behind. Although he had wanted to make the sale, he seemed like someone who had just left the funeral of a loved one. We chatted for a moment as friends, then he said "Well, guess I gotta go now" in a sorrowful tone. Knowing that land had been his life, I knew he would welcome some role to stay involved with it. I inquired "What are you going to do now Winn?" "Nothing," he replied. I got a quick idea.

Winn could usually be found in his car just sitting on the road for hours looking over his land. So I said, "We need someone to keep track of your land, if I give you a key to the gate could you help me out?" We didn't hug, but it was close! I also asked if he would spend a day and take me over every foot of the land and tell me what I should know about it. Winn remained a good friend to me and Refuge until his death a few years later. The Education Center was eventually built on a corner of this property, but more importantly it opened the flood-gates for more land purchases.

With the Nichols deed in my pocket, I visited L. Clark White at his home in Perry. He owned 380 acres of irrigated grasslands that was excellent wildlife habitat and had all kinds of potential for wet-land development. Clark was around 90, but got around fine. Still, he knew his time for ranching was coming to an end. A soft-spoken gentleman, Clark said he would rather sell to the Refuge than to any of his neighbors. You never know what you will uncover when you start talking to people. He had a long, unhappy relationship with neighbors and would rather see his land go to the Refuge. I spent some time with Clark in his pickup driving his landholdings and learning about how he managed his water rights. It was a cut-and-dried deal after that with an appraisal and an offer. He accepted and we closed shortly after that. Clark remained on friendly terms till his death years later. His property was a key unit in what would become the Grassland Habitat Unit (GHU) on the east side of the Refuge.

And so it went from there. The 114 acre Stauffer tract was also irrigated grassland and proved to be relatively easy to purchase. The land had been rented out on an annual basis for grazing and the current landowner had inherited it as a fraction of land from a larger ranch. Since it was generating minimal income, she was glad to have a fair market offer of cash on the barrel head. Sold. I was, of course, elated at this point at how the acquisitions were going.

The Duckville Club was an old-time waterfowl hunting club adjacent to the Refuge. Their 329 acre landholding contained a quaint clubhouse whose history went back to the turn of the 20th century. Long before road access, the clubhouse was built and accessed via floating the Bear River channel down from Corinne. One member, actor Wallace Beery, left a legacy of wild tales from the marsh and late nights in the clubhouse. The flood destroyed the clubhouse and left the membership with very limited hunting opportunity because their marsh was totally destroyed.

I decided to see how the Duckville Club would react to an offer to purchase their property, so I spoke with their manager "Shuse" Stingle. We hit it off right away. He was a no nonsense businessman and said if they got a fair offer the club would move north and purchase some land near Salt Creek. We had an offer prepared in short order and it was immediately accepted. Their 329 acre parcel fit perfectly into the north side of Unit 3.

That brought the total purchases in 1993 to 1,946 acres at a price of $852,806 or an average of $438 per acre. All the purchases were with Duck Stamp dollars. Go Duckstamps!

I continued contacting landowners on the far east side of the Refuge in what would become the Grassland Habitat Unit. Mim Davis held title to 256 acres. He was interested in an offer, so I requested an appraisal and paperwork for his purchase option. When making my follow-up visit I was told by his widow that he died while undergoing a "tummy tuck" operation. I gave her the paperwork and she decided to sell. This parcel tied up the land adjacent to the 1100 south interchange on I-15.

Anna Hall held a 40 acre parcel adjacent to the Davis tract on the north. She was a senior lady living on the grazing rent the land generated. It was a no-brainer for her to sell.

The Simpers held a 40 acre tract adjacent to the Davis tract on the south. The family was in the cattle business to some extent, but they lived in the Honeyville area. They decided to sell and reinvest the money in land closer to their main operation. It was a cut and dried deal. This property had a number of sheds and corrals. They were all removed shortly after the Refuge gained title.

That brought the total purchases in 1994 to 406 acres at a price of $247,000 or an average of $608 per acres. These tracts were also purchased with "Duck Stamp" dollars. As a highlight, I was selected to travel to Washington D.C. for the committee hearing to approve the sale (or not). The committee received more requests for land purchases than they had funds, so it was a competition for the money. It turned out to be an ego stroking time because my presentation was successful and others got turned down.

Later on, numerous other tracts were purchased one after another as I was able to make contact with landowners. Each transaction has its own story and I should not take space here to give that many details.

It is worth mentioning, though, that the single biggest purchase totaling over 6,000 acres was completed in 1995 from the Kundson family. Wow, that purchase was really difficult and took over 5 years of just plain old haggling over every boundary line, water right and smallest detail. I took part in negotiations on all the other tracts and it was an enjoyable process. We were straightforward and made the purchase agreement quickly. Not this time. The transaction was brokered through The Nature Conservancy, a non-profit support group that specializes in purchasing land quickly and reselling it to agencies. It makes sense because they can purchase land quickly with their funds and then hold the deed for months or even years while agencies work through red tape to appropriate funds to reimburse them. Dick Knuduson, the family negotiator, wanted an eventual deal but he just would not come to an agreement for a sale. I think Dick just enjoyed negotiating for its own sake. Sensing the process needed a big nudge (or more like a kick), I met with Chris Montigue, The Nature Conservancy negotiator, and told him we needed to press Knuduson for a deal or we were going to back away. That was a bold move because the Refuge really needed to make this deal. I drew a boundary of his landholdings that included the 6,000 acres and said we wanted all of it or none. Take it or leave it and we needed to know IMMEDIATELY so we could seek the funding. Eureka! Done deal. This tract added acreage to units 3,4, 5 and the Grassland Habitat Unit. A happy ending to a long, drawn out negotiation. Man oh man, that deal was a relief to complete!

By 1997, the total Grassland Habitat Unit acreage totaled 4,580 acres with 10 separate landowner tracts. Even more importantly, 22 new water rights were purchased with those lands enabling wetland habitats to be created. Exciting times!

The acquisition process as described above includes a lot of "I's", as in Al. That does not mean the success of the acquisition process was primarily due to me. The magic ingredient here was that Bob Valentine attained governor's approval for our program-- without it we would have not purchased one acre. Then the local corps of volunteers and Refuge supporters helped by placing the Refuge in a positive light for our neighboring landowners. It really made a difference because some landowners wanted their property to go to a positive cause. Everything about buying land from willing sellers requires a broad base of encouragement. And I got to see it all come together!

After 2002, one more major acquisition was made through a land trade/purchase in the east boundary of the Refuge near the 1100 south exit off I-15. In an area now known as Pointe Perry, a 'developer" from Idaho became interested in planning a shopping center on the site. Sparing you pages and pages of excruciating details, this man wooed Perry City into running utilities to the site and also secured other investors. Without public funds from Perry City, this stupid (I am trying to stay calm) development would not have been feasible. They intended to develop a corridor along the west side of Interstate 15 for over a mile. That would have had a huge impact on the Refuge. At my request, Bob Valentine was keeping the development at bay with his unique abilities to rally opposition from both Brigham City and Box Elder County. At one point, the developers were promising to get a Cabela's store. Big talkers. Hot air. All this publicity was not doing the Refuge any good, since we were being portrayed as spoilers. That was something we needed to avoid if possible.

I came up with a land trade/purchase proposal that would square off the development to include the area around the Interstate exchange AND exclude any further development. As part of the deal, the Refuge would gain title to a prime tract of irrigated grasslands as well as other surrounding grasslands. At the end of the day, we gained 200 acres and gave up 45. The transaction also stopped further development. It was the best we could do, but I still hate the sight of Pointe Perry. As a post script, the developer of Pointe Perry eventually let the bank take over the property, leaving Perry taxpayers and investors holding the bag.

When you wrap up the entire effort to purchase important lands for the Refuge, it was a great success. Newly purchased lands are now under permanent protection and will help provide a secure future for more wildlife. It was a very rewarding experience for everyone involved.

CHAPTER 17

THE FIRST BIG CONTRACTS

To reopen the Refuge to public use in 1990, the corps of volunteers completed all the work themselves or hired specific jobs to be completed with their own funds. They circumvented the typical government paperwork and procurement regulations by simply negotiating the best price and paying the vendor cash. That made work quick and simple. Not only that, if work was not done well you had to answer to the volunteers who were giving their time and resources for free. Needless to say, it was a good arrangement for getting work done well and on time.

In 1992, an appropriation was received to replace the old bridge decks the volunteers had previously raised from the river channel in 1990. They had sufficed for a time, but in the long run new concrete decks were needed. A contract went out calling for replacement decks that would be 2 feet wider than the originals. This new width would help with the wider requirements of bus and truck use. The contract also called for installing new steel radial gates at headquarters as well as Whistler and Reeder canals. Wadsworth Construction received the contract and completed the work satisfactorily.

Another contract was awarded to Butch Robinson to rebuild 20 miles of D-Line by adding 213,000 cubic yards of fill dirt. His work was accomplished with a dragline. This antiquated piece of machinery was a vestige from a bygone era. Butch kept it going by cannibalizing some old machines for spare parts. A few years later (1996 &1998) he was awarded the contract to excavate the Unit 3 drain and the Unit 5 drain. The old dragline was still going strong even though it left something to be desired for the way it looked, just like some of us old refuge managers.

Those contracts were eventually completed in a satisfactory manner, unlike the following two contracts that were a disaster.

In approximately 1997, we initiated planning to replace a shop building completely destroyed by the flood. An employee from the Regional Office Engineering took on the task of drawing the plans. That was mistake number one. The construction contract was awarded to a company named "Pro Controls." That was mistake number two. The company was not a legitimate construction company. It was headquartered in Washington D.C. and in business for the express purpose of bidding government projects then tangling up the contract with complaints, change orders and so forth. In our case, they initiated building the foundation to the wrong dimensions -even though they were issued a cease work order. When it was all said and done, they claimed $250,000 in damages for getting no work done. And worse yet, they were paid just to get them out of the contract. Poof, that was good money just lost to what I consider fraud. That stung bad and drove me nuts whenever I thought about it. I decided to do everything in my power to keep it from happening again, even though I didn't exactly know what I could do about it. You would think a government agency could protect itself from nonsense like that. Unfortunately, I have another bad example.

Al Trout

We had a cross dike to build in Unit 3 and time was wasting. It seemed like a good idea to issue a contract for a private company to do the work since our staff was fully engaged with building other dikes and water control structures. It was a simple job, just push up dirt and pack it down to make a dike. All large contracts were handled through a division of contracting in the Denver regional office. They were so-called experts and followed the zillions of rules regulating the contracting process. When the advertising period closed, the contract was awarded to Flynn Construction and it was another disaster. He was late getting started, did not perform up to standard and when he pulled out he requested a 20% bonus for hardship! I went nuts at the request, but it had to go to Regional Office Contracting for a decision. An inexperienced contracting officer buckled to the request. I went double nuts!! That kind of nonsense sets the tone for future contractors to do late and poor quality work.

We learned several things the hard way from this experience. Even though private contractors are supposed to be professionals and well experienced in the line of work, they often "juggle" several contracts at a time. This ensures they have plenty of work, even though it causes them to run late on some of their jobs. Since government contracts have built in safeguards for contractors, they delay government jobs to get private work done on time. Then our contracting division excuses the contractors for being late if they complain. I know, it shouldn't be that way but all of the laws and regulations in place keep guys like me from going out and firing a contractor not doing his job. Our contract administrators tended to be soft on contractors. That was sad, but true.

The Refuge environment also makes private contract work difficult. Refuge dirt work is different than anywhere else because the mudflat soil is unforgiving. If you make a mistake, your dozer or track hoe will sink to the cab before you can stop it. It takes experience and the right timing to get the job done. Refuge work usually comes down to getting lots of dirt moved in 30 days during the driest portion of the year. You have to be checking the site and move in promptly when conditions are right. Contractors don't keep tabs on the conditions and they don't give the Refuge priority scheduling. That means they miss critical scheduling windows and have to wait a year to try again. Not acceptable. Drives me crazy.

We also decided to avoid big contracts because they are really expensive. You might think that hard working private contractors (like my dad) could work circles around government people (think gravy train). Not at Bear River Refuge. Our guys took pride in their work and knew the environment on a daily basis. The core staff at the Refuge: Rich, Rod, Tim and Doug were dedicated and skilled at their jobs. They were the best and nobody could move dirt like they did. It was that simple. We saved a sizable portion of funds by doing work with our own staff or borrowing staff from other refuges for big jobs (refer to Chapter 24 "Just get 'er done.") Big contracts also required review by Engineering and Contracting offices. They sucked off over 20% of the funds just to approve the project. That is big money that was just lost from the Refuge budget. Finally, our own staff had to supervise and approve the work of contractors. That sounds easy, but in reality it took one of our maintenance staff off productive work just to make sure contractors were doing the job they were getting paid to do!

So, all in all, we opted not to use Engineering and Contracting unless we had no other choice. Instead we gave the work to our own staff and we saved big bucks. With the savings we purchased heavy equipment, more supplies and accomplished more work than expected. We saved enough to build the new shop, among other things.

It is a sad commentary, but the two branches of our agency who were supposed to help us, actually drove costs out the roof. We just avoided their *help* most of the time. Engineering told us what we already knew, and Contracting slowed down our procurement process and ensured we paid more than what it would cost locally. Sorry, but that's the truth. Well, I'm not really that sorry because we would have done better without them.

Having said those disparaging things about those segments of the Fish and Wildlife Service, I want to make it clear that the individual employees did their jobs as well as possible. They were simply constrained by a flawed organizational process.

CHAPTER 18

WATER RIGHTS, THE NUCLEAR OPTION

I first heard about water rights from my 7th grade western history teacher Mr. White. I immediately tuned him out because I was already fed up with civil rights, women's rights, animal rights and rights-of-way. "Now with water also wanting rights," I reasoned "what is next, coffee or tea?"

Over the course of my career, I was in for a rude awakening. My on-the-job training in water rights came from the school of hard knocks. Following is a brief background in some very basics of Utah water law I picked up along the way. Remember, I am not a lawyer and don't intend this to be a formal legal analysis. I just intend for the following comments to provide some perspective. If you would like more information, my advice is that you google Western water law and study to your heart's content.

When I arrived in Utah, I knew that water rights would be an issue. Flows in the Bear River are the lifeblood of the Refuge. The health of the Refuge would relate directly to an adequate water supply. With only a basic knowledge of Utah water rights, I thought it would be prudent to get better informed. Sure enough, I got the two basic axioms that form the basis of all water law and water management.

Axiom 1 states that water *sometimes* flows downhill. Axiom 2 states that water *always* flows toward money. I also learned another important fact: an unidentified group of individuals is involved and influential in water law and water development. They are referred to as the "water buffaloes." No, they don't wear name tags. And yes, they probably have an unflattering label for me. I had a healthy fear and respect for the water buffaloes because they knew their stuff and had political connections.

I'm not a lawyer (obviously), but I would like to lay out a very big picture perspective of water law in Utah. If you are not a born and bred westerner, the system of laws regulating water in this part of the country may seem strange. Well they are strange, but there is a reason for it.

As the frontier moved from the water-abundant eastern states to the much drier climate of the West in the 1800's, a shift in water law doctrine was made. This basic shift was from the Eastern riparian doctrine which gave landowners the right to use surface water adjacent to their land, but it fell short of granting them the right to own the water separate from the land as real property.

In contrast, under the Western doctrine of prior appropriations, Utah grants ownership of water to individual water users through a legal process. Water right applicants must prove they have diverted the water out of its source, like a spring, river or lake and consumed it to accomplish a "beneficial use." Here is the clincher: water rights are granted on a first come first served basis and are considered real property which can be bought and sold at will, even apart from the land.

Yes! You too can own the water in a river or lake. This may sound like a TV add, but it is true. During the early settlement years of the arid West, this system was appropriate. It helped attract people to the wilderness. Problem is, it has the ultimate effect of dewatering the water courses in an already dry climate. It actually encourages the reduction of flows in rivers across the West. Shouldn't we be trying to save what is left of our streams instead of encouraging their decline? Stupid question.

With that perspective, I knew the future of the Refuge depended on our success in the arena of water rights. Whatever water we were not able to protect under the Refuge right would one day be removed from the river and sent to "the money" (probably industry or suburbia). That thought was a downright fright.

The Refuge held a Utah water right issued in 1928 that specified we could divert a flow of up to 1,000 cubic feet per second (cfs) out of the Bear River. That sounds specific, but the water right certificate did not give the maximum amount of water that could be taken over the course of the year. In other words, we knew how big of a flow we could take, but we didn't know what legal limit would be put on the volume. That volume, measured in acre/feet, is the amount of water it takes to cover one acre of land one foot deep. It may seem hard to believe that the total yearly volume in the Refuge water right had not been legally determined, but that was a big question waiting to be answered. It was a difficult number to come up with because flows in the Bear River fluctuate extensively throughout the year. Sometimes the river would reach a spring high of possibly 3,000 cubic feet per second, then crash to less than 100 cubic feet per second by August.

To determine just exactly how big your annual slice of the water pie should be, Utah law puts the responsibility of recording yearly water use on the individual with the water right. Someone from the state does not do it for you. Diverting water onto your land for a useful purpose is called beneficial use. The amount of water put to beneficial use will be used by Utah officials to set the volume limit on the water right.

It is one thing for a farmer to document water used for irrigation by going to a single point of diversion where the water is taken from a canal and sent down a ditch to the fields. It was quite another problem for the Refuge to "prove," or even know, how much water from the Bear River was intentionally diverted for wildlife management when the whole river channel spills into the Refuge. I know what you are thinking! The answer is NO, you can't just say the whole river counts as beneficial use for the Refuge. Water courts don't work that way. You must show how much water was intentionally put to use for the purpose of wildlife. That is a hard order to put your arms around. Question is, just how do you prove the amount of water needed for waterfowl and 200 other species of birds over the course of the year? There were no simple formulas to calculate Refuge water needs that could be defended in court if necessary.

It boils down to the fact that the Refuge has received a "free lunch" from the Bear River because it is located at river's end and the Refuge had use of all the incoming water, even though a good portion of it was in excess to the Refuge water right. That was good news up until now. We got use of a lot of water that did not legally belong to us just because it was there. And it was there because the people who held the water right had no infrastructure upstream of the Refuge to get it out. The State of Utah owns the largest portion of Bear River water, but getting to it by funding the construction of a big dam or diversion structure has been out of the question. It is a downright fright to wonder how soon it may become economically feasible.

When developers eye the river for water, the only "developable" flows are contained in the spring runoff, which hit the Bear River in April, May and June, prior to irrigation demands. In order to tap that source of water, it would have to be retained by a large dam. That expense is not justified for agricultural use because farming is not lucrative enough to pay the cost of dams, canals and other infrastructure. If built, it would have to be for municipal uses. That means moving the water south toward Salt Lake City.

With Utah's population heading upward like a rocket, state planners have their eye on the Bear River for helping urbanize the remaining space along the Wasatch Front. Yippee. Sorry, I just think developing every square inch between Tremonton and Spanish Fork is going to degrade our state, not improve it. Anyway, state leaders began seeking analysis of all possible reservoir sites along the Bear River. The goal was to impound all of Utah's share of the Bear River. That effort, led by a legislative appointed committee, "The Bear River Task Force," sent water engineers combing the entire length of the river channel for suitable sites for building a dam.

There are few things that are harder to stomach than engineers who are filled with joy about finding new places to dam one of the very few remaining rivers in the West. Those engineers came back to the committee with at least five sites that would work from their standpoint -as long as they were given a HUGE check from the public coffers. They could hardly contain themselves because opportunities to build large dams anywhere in the West are very rare to non-existent. The vast majority of rivers are already dammed up. But here they were, licking their chops at the Bear River. Too good to be true. Kind of like being famous for killing the last wild buffalo. They had the Bear River in the crosshairs and their finger was on the trigger.

So there we sat, with proposals for dams up and down the Bear River. Then came the question, just how much water *exactly* could Utah plan on extracting from the river? To answer that, all water users would be required to have both a maximum diversion rate and an annual volume specified in their water right. Add up all those rights, subtract them from the total annual flows and presto, you get the acre/ feet of water you could legally remove from the river. In this case, the "excess" water would be captured by a dam in the spring and then sent via canal or pipeline to anywhere along the Wasatch Front or beyond. The thought of that makes me ill, but politicians and developers will tell you "God would have done it in the first place if He would have had the funding."

Well, you guessed it, the Refuge received a notice from Utah Water Rights requiring we file for both a rate and total volume of annual water use. For the Refuge, that required a diversion-by-diversion breakdown as well as an acre-by-acre area of use. That is a BIG DEAL. A really BIG DEAL. How do you show intentional water use on a 70 square mile area crisscrossed with channels, depressions, marsh, mudflat and the like? I had no idea. If I had no idea and the Fish and Wildlife Service had no idea, then the Utah Departments of Water Rights and Water Resources would be able to make their own determinations and minimize our water needs. This was not a good idea because wildlife management is not universally recognized as a beneficial use in the Utah water rights world.

This was a potential crisis for the Refuge. Nothing is more important than the water supply. You can have all the land you want, but if the water is taken you have no migratory birds. Get this, God was about to provide the next "hero" for the Refuge. Enter Bob Green from the Denver Regional Office. He held the Chief position of Water Resources. I didn't know it, but I was about to get an education in the world of water rights from a true master.

First, Bob negotiated for a time extension until February 1993 for the Refuge to put together an extensive list of what water rights we were to claim. The Fish and Wildlife Service subsequently submitted four claims. Included was a *Federal Reserved right* for 2,544 cfs with a volume of 481,432 acre/feet annually. The other three claims included a filing on the "basic" state granted water right of 1928 and then we added two additional smaller "diligence" claims.

Kerpow!! That filing fell like an atomic bomb. First, it was way BIGGER than Utah expected. And second, it included the Federal Reserved claim. Notice the word "Federal": that meant we were claiming a huge chunk of the river apart from any state process. It was saying in essence, "Because Congress established the Refuge, they automatically intended that it have adequate water. We say this much is the adequate amount." Utah HATED that with a passion because it takes that water completely out of their authority to regulate in any way.

Looking back, this is kind of funny. Nobody from the Utah Water Rights knew the Service was even considering the assertion of a Federal Reserved right in addition to the basic 1928 Utah water right. They found out when they opened the mail one fine day and read our filing. Here is the funny part. I was dumb as a post regarding how extreme the filing was and what it would do to upset the world of water rights. The water buffaloes were about to stampede!

Everything was quiet for a few weeks; then I decided to attend a water conference-- "the Bear River Water Quality Symposium"-- just to keep up the Refuge presence among all the players involved in Bear River planning. Well, Dave, the manager of the Bear River Canal Company, had become aware of our filing (it was public information) and decided to create some hype. ("thanks, Dave".) Although not on the agenda, he stood up and announced he had copies of the Refuge filing and dispersed them to everyone--probably about 200 folks. He then gave a quick speech telling everyone how extreme and dangerous the filing was to other water users in Utah. He, of course, exaggerated the situation and it worked for him. Up until that time, I got used to dealing with support from up and down the spectrum of agencies and people. That all changed in a matter of minutes. I was identified as an adversary and my refuge manager world was turned upside down immediately.

For the next six months the Refuge water right was the subject of newspapers, television, radio and other publications. With backlash coming on a daily basis, just keeping a lid on things consumed my entire schedule. I was most concerned this issue would spill over into our land purchase efforts and halt any new acquisition. Good will was hard to find right then.

To my rescue came Bob Valentine. He was my perfect hero for the issue. Since he was connected from Box Elder County to Utah State Government and on to Washington D.C. (Congressman Hansen, Senators Hatch and Bennett) he was uniquely able--and willing--to get the hype cooled down. I briefed Bob on what had happened and he personally made contacts up and down the line to assure people we would get through this in an acceptable manner. Whoever had such a friend on the sidelines, willing to help whenever you called? Bob never flinched in his support and he didn't second guess the logic behind the filing of the federal reserved claim. I was truly blessed!

As an immediate remedy, Bob called for a meeting with Bob Morgan. He was head of Utah Water Rights. Valentine led a very productive discussion that centered on clarifying issues and seeking a solution. It would have been impossible for me to fill that role since I was an agency guy. Valentine, however, held a considerable sway because he had been Director of the Division of Wildlife Resources a few years prior and worked with Bob Morgan during those years. That meeting was an important turning point in the controversy.

Although most concerned people settled down, Bear River Water Conservancy District manager, Frank, kept coordinating as much opposition as he could through the Governor's office and Washington. He even kept it up with Wyoming and Idaho officials. Our Regional Director Ralph Morgenweck received a phone call at home on Sunday morning from the Governor of Wyoming requesting he remove the Federal Reserved Right! To Ralph's credit, he held tight with the filing as submitted. Frank delivered his biggest jab by eroding congressional support for an appropriation we were seeking through the "Land and Water Conservation Fund," or LWCF. This fund contains tax revenues from boat fuel and offshore oil drilling for use in conservation work. Losing our chance to receive LWCF money that year was a blow to our land acquisition. We had no choice left but to seek Duck Stamp funds, a much smaller and highly competitive source of money.

We needed to resolve the water rights issue as quickly as possible because the Refuge restoration and expansion were coming under fire. We needed support from everyone, not an ongoing battle. The issue had two elements, legal and hydrological. To solve the legal issue, the Fish and Wildlife withdrew the Federal Reserved Water Right claim with a commitment by the state of Utah to secure the water we needed through the regular state legal framework.

The second issue was hydrology. That is, we needed to be able to substantiate just how much water we needed throughout the year and why. Bob Green, who would later become a full time volunteer, took the lead on this effort. With his guidance, we began fleshing out a "Long Term Water Management Plan." It was based on bird use in each of the 27 management units identified in the ultimate development goal. The "Long Term Water Management Plan" spelled out wildlife objectives and the habitat needed to reach those objectives. Total Refuge water needs were then calculated by determining how much water was needed to create and maintain that habitat on a daily basis. Wew, quite a process but it gave us a leg to stand on in Utah court if we needed to justify the amount of water in our filing.

As it turned out, our total water needs exceeded 400,000 acre/feet per year. A hefty sum of water, it was enough to cover each acre of marsh by about 10 feet. Our documentation was so thorough that state officials did not question our final numbers. It was a great reward for a lot of staff work.

As the shock of our water filing began to wear off and it became evident the Refuge was going to get a fair slice of the Bear River, Larry Anderson, Director of the Utah Department of Water Resources offered a "deal we couldn't refuse." He proposed a partnership for building a dam near Honeyville and splitting the water 50-50 between Utah and the Refuge. The dam would store 100,000 acre/feet of water and the Refuge would get half of that to be released whenever we wanted--probably mid-summer. HUMMMM. Well, "Ok. Let's put a proposal together and see if we can get buy-in from Washington," I replied. After a huge amount of work over a year's time, Cheryl Willis (our Chief of Water Resources) and I made a presentation in Washington D.C. pitching the project. Surprisingly, we got concurrence to move ahead with planning. Shock, shock, shock. The Fish and Wildlife Service *never* supports damming rivers-- until now. Delivering 50,000 Ac/Ft of water to the Refuge would be a HUGE benefit to wildlife in the dry summer months. We also assumed that habitat damage from the footprint of the dam would be fully mitigated as the project was built. I came back to Utah feeling like a successful salesman. Look at me go in my suit and tie!

If you haven't noticed, there is no Honeyville dam on the Bear River today. "What happened?" you ask. I came back to Utah after gaining approval to move ahead and contacted Larry Anderson right away. I thought he would be elated with the good news. Instead, he sheepishly replied, "I did not expect you get approval to partner with us." Larry went on to say he suggested the project because it made him "look good" to the public and he expected us to say no. "I planned to use this against the Refuge for not wanting to partner with us" he explained. That short conversation killed the project.

I was completely flabbergasted. Larry had just cost the Refuge thousands of dollars in travel and nearly one staff/year of time for nothing. I later got an apology from Dennis, his assistant, but Larry never showed any remorse for trying to set me up. The water rights issue cooled down for a while after that as Utah worked behind the scenes to finalize all the other water rights claims on the river. Like most issues in the public realm, new stories get lots of attention from the press. The public becomes disinterested over time and reporting comes to a halt.

Later on, in the year 2000, I was approached by our Bureau of Reclamation friends regarding another possible source of water for the Refuge. They operated Hyrum Dam, located in Cache Valley a few miles upstream on a tributary of the Bear River. They recommended raising the existing Dam to gain 50,000 acre/feet of storage that could go entirely to the Refuge whenever we wanted. And NO, Utah was not included in this deal--just the Refuge. It was a great proposal. The Bureau was willing to do all the physical work on the dam, they just needed a big appropriation from Congress. For the "average" refuge that would be a killer right there. Most refuges don't have enough influence or support in Congress to garner an appropriation that large.

But we had Bob Valentine, and he went right to work on our behalf and talked to Congressman Jim Hansen and Senator Bob Bennett. Over the months of planning and design, we kept Bob in the middle of the process. As you can guess, everyone comes out of the shadows as a proposal like this becomes public and it gains momentum. That was Bob's strength, he could speak to every group or agency and keep the project moving ahead. At the end of the day, we gave up a small percentage of storage water to an irrigation district to gain their approval and "seal the deal."

Congressman Hansen took the lead and had full funding for this project added into a larger proposal, called the "Cal-Fed Bill." We were just a small part of this huge bill authorizing over a billion dollars of projects. Whoppee! For the first time the Refuge was going to benefit from a large water bill. As we waited in anticipation for this huge windfall, the fiscal year dragged on and on and on. Congress was in deadlock, nothing was being introduced for debate. So finally, the fall arrived with no action in the Senate and all pending bills just died. DANG, what a way to lose. I was angry; that was the first congressional "deadlock" that I had heard of. Sadly, it would not be the last as it became more common place in the political system. But then and there, I was angry and blamed the Senate Majority leader Tom Daschle. In all reality, it was probably a much more complex issue than just one man holding up all the bills. It is just that we had come so close to obtaining a summer water source for the Refuge that I could taste success. I was looking for a fat lady to sing. Unfortunately, I was guilty of counting my chicks before they hatched!

As time passed, the water rights issue slowly became less hostile. The state of Utah accepted the fact the Refuge had a substantial water right that could be legally defended. Working through the channels of state law would take time, but Refuge water rights had been filed and a proper defense made for the amount claimed.

In finalizing the process, all the proposed water right claims in a defined area are published for public information. A comment or protest period follows, giving time opportunity for claims to be challenged. If challenged, a claim may be negotiated to a mutually agreeable solution or settled legally. At the end of this process, each user receives an approved water right and is listed in a book. This process on the Bear River has taken decades and it is still not finalized for the Refuge at the time of this writing.

With all that said, I still want the Refuge to have the whole dang river! Seems to me that the process would be fast and fair if we could just go to Judge Judy or be on *Hot Bench.*

CHAPTER 19

WHERE DID THE MEANDERLINE GO? -OR WHO REALLY OWNS THE REFUGE?

Back before Utah became a State (1898), the Federal government sent surveyors to plot the boundary of Great Salt Lake. Reason being, permanent lakes (think "Great Lakes") remained in ownership of the Federal Government even though they were within state borders. The boundaries of these public bodies of water were determined by surveyors who plotted the shore line encircling the normal high water line. Sounds simple, right? But no, establishing a meander line (or normal high water level) around Great Salt Lake proved more than the Federal government could accomplish in those years.

It's not like the feds didn't try. Survey parties were sent out, which was a major trek itself in those days before any roads. Once here, Federal surveyors weren't exactly welcomed by the local residents who held a low level of trust for everyone related to the Federal government (that is an understatement). One party of surveyors would come out, do as much surveying as possible and leave without having completed the lake boundary. Likewise, other survey parties came out, did a partial job and left. This went on over the years. The end product was a map with incomplete lines and various gaps. Even worse, the lines that were plotted were not the same elevation. It was a hodgepodge product at best.

Let's give the surveyors a break. Plotting the lake's shoreline at a static elevation was impossible because the shoreline was constantly moving up or down. The bed underlying Great Salt Lake is so flat; it has a slope of only one foot per mile. So, even an inch rise in the lake's level would move the shoreline in or out more than 400 feet. Since it has no outlet and inflowing rivers and streams vary greatly according to annual snowpack, the lake's depth changes continually. It goes up with the snowmelt in spring and down as the intense summer sun evaporates 60 inches of water off its surface in an average year. Several dry years in a row take their collective toll on the lake's elevation and a string of wetter than normal years brings the shoreline to flood levels. There really is no "normal high water line" that could possibly be surveyed by a crew on foot using the survey equipment of the time. You just can't get the lake to "hold still" long enough to get a line circumventing the entire shoreline that would represent one elevation. Pesky lake!

That left the boundary of Great Salt Lake in contention for decades. Even lacking a good survey, the federal government held on to control of Great Salt Lake after Utah gained statehood. When the Refuge became established in 1928, its 64,500 acre footprint covered private land, federal land and state lands. Title was gained through what was thought to be proper legal channels and all was well with the Refuge land titles until the early 1970's. That is when Utah first challenged the U.S. ownership of Great Salt Lake. In a surprise turn of events, the U.S. Supreme Court announced they would consider land dispute cases from individual states. BINGO, an attorney's dream come true! Utah jumped on that opportunity and was invited to argue its case for ownership of the entire Great Salt Lake. What a joke, right? Well, guess what, Utah won! As for the Refuge, it was not affected because Utah expressly excluded the Refuge lands from their lawsuit, so the status quo was not disturbed as far as the Refuge was concerned. It was a live-and-let-live attitude between Utah and the Refuge, at least for a while. Decades passed and the issue was all but forgotten, or so I thought.

I was dumb and happy one day in 2000 when I heard the fax machine start up. The machine printed out a "letter of intent to sue" from the State of Utah. It put the Fish and Wildlife Service on notice that Utah believed they owned the lands under the Refuge and they intended to take us to court. WHAT?? You have got to be joking. Why now? And what do we do?

Seems that when the Fish and Wildlife Service filed for water rights (see Chapter 18), the exertion of a "Federal Reserved Water Right" struck fear into Utah's water regulatory agencies--and all the way up to the governor's office. As Utah assembled their lawyers, they searched for legal reasons to shoot down the claim. It occurred to their lawyers that a Federal Reserved water right can only be filed on lands that are owned by the federal government. Well, well. If Utah could win the argument for owning the lands within the Refuge boundaries, it would nullify the Federal Reserved claim. GULP. They could use their same argument as presented to the Supreme Court for owning Great Salt Lake proper. It worked once, they thought it may work again. I wasn't sure, but I did know that going to court takes a lot of time and effort. Outcome in court is also uncertain, the outcome is never guaranteed.

Our legal team, led by Department of Interior lawyers also went to work. They concluded that Utah had a case, but not a slam dunk. The Federal defense would pivot around the argument that Utah had allowed the Feds to spend millions on the Refuge over the years. Furthermore, Utah had cooperated in many ways over management programs. Utah even traded land to the Federal government that they were now claiming title to! U.S. lawyers held to the argument that Utah could not make an about face at this point in time over their claim on the lakebed. That, of course, is a simplified version of the case, but suffice it to say our Department legal team was going to give it a good fight. Oh, one other tidbit.

The legal team for Utah was led by "Steve", the son of the Utah lawyer who argued Utah's case to the Supreme Court for ownership of Great Salt Lake. That victory was a major legal trophy. And now son Steve was chomping at the bit to follow-up nearly 30 years later for his own "day in court."

These complex issues have several sides: political, legal and managerial. Government legal teams are supposed to be controlled by agency Directors and authorities. However, in this case Utah lawyers had ran ahead and taken the lead. Problem is lawyers do legal work and like to go to court. Pending legal actions hanging overhead do not usually encourage on—the-- ground solutions. Lawyers like to dictate agency procedure, and it seldom works toward a friendly out-of-court resolution between two reasonable agencies. Lawyers just don't usually make good managers (my humble opinion). As we were becoming consumed with the legal aspect of this issue, Kathleen Clark was appointed Director of Utah's Department of Natural Resources. Kathleen was sharp, strong and resolution oriented. She had a commonsense approach to solving problems. And best of all, I had a history with Kathleen that dated back to 1990 when she was on staff with Congressman Jim Hansen. We were on friendly ground with a healthy dose of mutual respect. We even liked each other. Well, at least I liked her.

To stop the lawyers from "sabre rattling" so something could actually be done to resolve the issue, Kathleen proposed a meeting with her staff, the Refuge (me) and representatives from Interior. Right off the get-go Kathleen took control. She let it be known she was in charge. She invited Utah lawyers to lay out the case so everyone understood Utah's legal issues clearly. Then came the good part that made me smile; in one fell swoop Kathleen told the lawyers to leave the meeting. We would be discussing all possibilities for resolution. That included alternatives of not going to court. She made it clear that the lawyers were working for her, their days of driving the process were over. Yea Kathleen! I love good leadership.

The U.S. asserted that Utah had no standing to claim Refuge lands because the meander line was incomplete within the vicinity of the Refuge. Therefore, Utah could not just arbitrarily fill in a meander line border since it was never formally established. At Refuge establishment in 1928, all public lands within the Refuge boundary were legally "reserved" from the public domain, meaning they were retained in permanent ownership of the Department of Interior. Another 18,000 acres were acquired by purchase from private landowners and by trading land with the State of Utah. To create another tangle, some of the lands were acquired from the railroad land grants. Sound complicated and a bit confusing? It is. It means that Utah was opening a can of worms and the outcome was anything but certain – for Utah or the Fish and Wildlife Service. One thing for sure: it would keep lawyers busy for years to come!

When Congressman Hansen was briefed on the issue, he proposed a whole new solution. He offered to seek funds from a special legal settlement fund (an unknown source to almost anyone you talk to) that is set aside for issues like this. So, it came down to our Regional Director, Ralph Morgenweck, negotiating directly with Kathleen Clark to reach a settlement agreement for a $15 million payment to

Utah. Utah would then issue a "Quit Claim Deed" for all Refuge lands – including future expansion lands that may be purchased by the Refuge. A legal line would then be established to declare that the Refuge will be considered above the meander line for good. That would put the issue to bed permanently. I'll bet the lawyers were none too happy over this issue being settled out of court.

The agreement was finalized and Secretary of Interior Norton made a special trip to Salt Lake City to sign on behalf of the U.S. Governor Leavitt signed on behalf of Utah. It was my pleasure to attend and watch as two high level authorities signed an agreement that affected me directly. I had the best job because after the ceremony I went back to the Refuge. All the other players went back to desk jobs!

One other thing, the meeting was held a few days after the terrorist attack on September 11, 2001. Secretary Norton was told to fly out here VIA airlines to help show the general public that it was safe to fly again.

Why should the Federal government have to "buy back" lands that it already owns? Isn't that a waste of money? After all, $15 million is a lot of money and it seems like Utah is just taking the Feds for a ride. Congressman Hansen was aware of that argument, so his solution was House Bill H.R. 3958 "Bear River Migratory Bird Refuge Improvement Act of 2002". The bill was to appropriate $15 million, but specified that $10 million was to be deposited into an account entitled "Wetlands and Habitat Protection Account". The account was to be administered by a Board of Directors with the goal of enhancing the wetlands around Great Salt Lake. Further guidelines protected the principal in perpetuity, allowing only the annual proceeds to be spent for wetlands projects. This was truly a win-win for wetlands, a rarity in politics.

The prospect of having a large fund set aside for wetlands really had me pumped. It seemed as though this resolution was a done deal.

Unfortunately, the agreement went south when someone far up the chain of command decided it would be better off not to go through with it. That brings the issue back into the realm of being settled through legal channels. It can be expected to take decades and many staff years for both the U.S. government and Utah state government to settle. In my humble opinion it will cost the Fish and Wildlife Service nearly as much in legal costs as the proposed settlement offer. When the federal government butts heads with state governments it is usually a slow and expensive process. If it is ever settled in court in favor of Utah, the money awarded to Utah will not go into a wetland and habitat protection fund.

CHAPTER 20

THE PRIVATE LANDS INITATIVE

The whole idea of working on private lands was a foreign concept to many of the "old timers" working on refuges. We were an agency that worked totally on our own lands. My old heroes were hands-on people who had farming backgrounds. They could get the job done with little more than basic farm equipment and a shop with the most basic of tools and equipment. All their work was done behind the refuge boundary signs. That was true from the 1930's through the 1970's.

In reality, most species of wildlife rely on private lands at least part of the time. As important as refuges are, more wildlife actually depend on private lands for existence. Landowners simply control more lands (by far) than refuges and are able to maintain more acres of habitat across a large area.

Trouble was, our funding from Congress was specific for use on refuge owned lands. More refuge managers in my era recognized the need to work with private landowners to develop habitat on privately owned farms and ranches. The relentless destruction of wildlife habitat on private land was just an ugly fact of life. Somehow the trend needed to be reversed.

As with most complex problems that don't have an easy solution, a grassroots leader emerges with a solution and is willing to spend a great deal of effort to get it implemented. Such was the case of how the Private Lands Program began with the Fish and Wildlife Service. Rick Dornfeld and Carl Madsen, in the upper Midwest initiated a simple concept. Simply make a common-sense deal with a private landowner and help cost-share the project. The completed work must be an advantage to both the landowner and wildlife. It may be as simple as fencing around a prairie wetland to keep cattle from overgrazing and mucking up the pond. A culvert is placed to convey water from the pond to a trough for cattle. The area is transformed into excellent wildlife habitat. It provides clean water for the cattle and more habitat for wildlife. WIN-WIN. You close the deal with a handshake and share the expenses for the project. A simple contract specifies the details and guarantees the project will remain in place.

That is the gist of the program. Simple and effective. Rick and Carl paved the way by implementing projects and honing the process. With good success, they were able to get the attention of decision makers, and the "Private Lands Program" became officially sanctioned. Soon it became a budget item and began to be spread across the Nation.

It took some sacrifice on the part of each refuge to begin private lands work because additional employees were not provided to do the work. It was a matter of taking time with existing staff to make contacts and develop projects. That initial work is time consuming and not always successful, but you just keep after it if you are committed to the concept. That is what we did. Our first private landowner contacts were made by Mark Lanier (asst. manager) and Vicki Hirschboeck (biologist). We completed some wetland enhancement projects with interested landowners and demonstrated our commitment to the Private Lands Program. So, overtime we were on the Regional Office's list for getting a "Private Lands Coordinator" position if and when funding would trickle down from Washington.

In a short time, the Private Lands Program grew to the point that positions were being funded across the country. We ranked high because we were maintaining a basic private lands program with Refuge staff alone. I got the word from Rick Dornfeld, who had been promoted into the position of Regional Private Lands Supervisor in the Denver office that we would receive funding to hire a new staff position. It would be wholly dedicated to growing the Private Lands Program in Utah. I was thrilled, knowing that there is a huge potential for private lands projects around the Bear River drainage and beyond.

This is a prime example of how the staff grew over the years. We helped each other expand into new responsibilities that were outside the "official job duties." Good things were accomplished and additional funding eventually followed. We did not use the excuse that we were not paid to do the extra work. The staff was willing to go above and beyond to keep our ever expanding program on the move.

I looked over the applicants for Private Lands Coordinator and chose the person who had the best qualifications and references. Karl Fleming was the choice, a man I had never met. His background experience was from Lake Andes, South Dakota--a station I served at between 1974 and 1978. I knew the area was a great proving ground for private lands work and Karl got good reviews from his supervisor.

Karl arrived on duty in May of 1998 and took off like a rocket at the new job. I was more than pleased at every aspect of his work. He related well with private landowners, and they responded to him. He had a commonsense approach that was extremely successful. Some of his best work was with landowners who bordered the Refuge. Some were hunt clubs, like the Canadian Goose Club and Bear River Club, that controlled large acreages of managed wetlands. Karl's contacts with them helped foster a cooperative relationship that benefited the "big picture" of habitat. Members from both of those clubs contributed substantially to the construction of the Education Center and later for the educational programs.

In 1999 alone, Karl completed 19 private lands projects across the state. He has continued at the helm of this program even at the time of this writing. One person, working independently, can make a difference. The Utah Private Lands program is a direct fruit of Karl's hard work and abilities.

Another key player and innovator in the Private Lands Program was Terry Messmer, a professor at Utah State University. Originally from Mott, North Dakota, a small town in Southwest North Dakota, Terry had a farm background prior to his education in wildlife biology. He had a strong belief that partnerships between various agencies and private landowners were the key to the future of wildlife management. Terry and I hit it off right away. I liked developing partnerships to get things done on the ground and so did Terry. We developed a deep bond of trust. It was just a matter of time before we entered into some partnership agreements between Utah State University and the Refuge. Highlighting our partnership was a written agreement essentially letting me use Terry as a sort of "bank" for Refuge funds that had to be spent by a certain date. I could obligate those to our agreement and then retrieve them later on when the time was right. That let me get the most bang for the buck. It helped me avoid the fiscal year spending spree. In a sense, Terry was my banker! Now you won't find that in the black and white instruction manual. We just put our creative juices together and got the job done. It helped us spend our limited budgets more efficiently. Even though we were working outside the box, I never lost a minute of sleep because we were benefitting the cause. I loved that kind of stuff, can't you tell?

As a sort of fringe benefit, Terry knew where some of the nation's best pheasant hunting was in the area around his hometown. A group of his associates traveled back to his boyhood prairies and I joined them once. We had an absolutely wonderful time just kicking back together in the evenings after a vigorous day in the field. No, we did not charge off the expenses to our government accounts. We just had a plain and simple good time.

CHAPTER 21

HUNTING AND LAW ENFORCEMENT

The Refuge has a long, famous history of public hunting. The hunting tradition started well before the 1928 establishment of the Refuge. Dating back even to the visit of John Fremont in 1848, his journal says he dined on a meal of plovers the evening he first arrived at the delta of the Bear River – now the very heart of the Refuge. As settlers arrived in the 1850's, the abundant flocks were harvested for a local food source. When the golden spike was driven in 1869, it provided rail connections to game markets in Denver and Sacramento. Thus, the era of market hunting began and a greatly expanded hunt was sustained for profit by professional hunters. It seems that even with the added kill from market hunting, the great flocks of waterfowl were not depleted. However, in 1890 unrelated events on the river would, through cause and effect, deal a major blow to waterfowl numbers.

An irrigation company built a diversion dam upstream on the Bear River a few miles north of the delta. The diversion fed a series of canals that carried off a flow of up to 1,000 cubic feet per second from the river (the equivalent of 2,000 acre/feet per day). That water went to soak thousands of acres of thirsty croplands and create a vibrant agricultural industry – a noble cause in itself, but dealing a death blow to the downstream marshes in the river's delta.

The natural marshes in the delta area were strangled of water throughout the summer and the vast acreage of marshes shrank to several thousand acres – a small fraction of their former size. Yet, the tradition of hunting survived through the efforts of hunter/conservationists. The Bear River Club was established in 1898 and was among the first to begin the work of marsh restoration. They pioneered the process of building dikes within the vast mudflats of Bear River Bay. Using water rights from the Malad River, they diverted precious flows into their club and reestablished thousands of acres of top quality marshes. Other clubs carved out landholdings in the area, built dikes and began managing wetlands to hold and attract migrant birds for hunting. Clubs such as "Duckville" and "Chesapeake" became established along with a host of other smaller clubs. Land ownership was a patchwork of private, state and federal. The general public found ample area to hunt on the State and Federal lands while some people chose to join the private clubs. There was an opportunity for everyone.

Concurrently, the migratory flocks were jammed into the overall shrinking acres of habitat because total waterflows to the delta were being depleted by irrigation diversions. The tipping point finally came in the early 1900's. For the first time in recorded history, botulism ran rampant throughout the great flocks and millions of waterfowl succumbed to the bacterial disease. It was ugly. The death toll reached into the millions of birds over the next few years and it seemed unstoppable. Hunters were alarmed at the sudden decline in waterfowl numbers and began a grassroots effort to establish a refuge for the express purpose of rebuilding the lost marsh habitats. Thus, the idea behind Bear River Migratory Bird Refuge was conceived. From the very start, hunters were involved with the grassroots effort to establish the Refuge and replenish the marshes.

From those local efforts, Bear River Migratory Bird Refuge was established by an Act of Congress in 1928. Those supporters were keenly interested in the future of hunting on the area. An agreement was written, as part of the Refuge establishment paperwork that specified 40% of the flooded area of the Refuge would be opened to public hunting. The state of Utah helped seal the deal by issuing the Refuge its own water right from the river for 1,000 cubic feet per second.

Construction was started on a network of 50 miles of dikes and 50 water control structures. These were designed to divert and impound the flows of the Bear River. By the early 1930's, construction was complete and Bear River Refuge began impounding flows from the river and managing water levels to improve waterfowl habitat. It was a great success and an example of the newly emerging science of Wildlife Management. Since construction was nearly complete, it was ready for operation and was officially declared open for "administration."

The Refuge specified hunting areas totaling a little over 12,000 acres open to the public. It was an instant success and through the next decades proved to be the most successful public hunting area in this region of the West. Records were kept as each hunter had to check in and check out and show all harvested birds to Refuge personnel. Access to the marshes was limited to a few locations and regulations were strictly enforced. All guns were checked for magazine plugs, limiting the firearm to 3 shells and hunters had to produce their hunting licenses and "duck stamps" each time they entered.

As the traditional sport of "water fowling" was passed from generation to generation over the ensuing decades, it was brought to a sudden halt by mother nature herself in 1983 when a flood of 100 year proportions arrived- one inch at a time. The slowly rising waters of Great Salt Lake totally engulfed the Refuge, topped the dikes, flowed into the diked off headquarters buildings and brought all Refuge operations to an end. Salt water killed all marsh vegetation and virtually wiped out waterfowl use. The hunting program was suspended past the boundary signs which were posted on D-Line, the southernmost Refuge dike.

As floodwaters receded, portions of the hunting zones were posted so they could once again be opened to hunting. However, with little or no vegetation, hunting use was minimal in the late 1980's and early 1990's. Reposting the hunt areas was all done by volunteers in those years, led by Bob Ebeling himself.

The long term plan for hunting was set during the writing of the Environmental Assessment of 1992, authored by Keith Hansen. During the public meetings we listened to input from the public and hunters who wanted to know what our plans were. During this process, we laid out a plan to acquire more land for the Refuge – thousands of acres in both purchased lands and lands protected through easements. Question was, how much would be opened if and when we bought more land? The answer- we would open the same proportion of new lands to hunting as was agreed to with the established Refuge. In other words, 40%. That answer was accepted and never debated as being fair. Both hunters and non- hunters alike could live with it because it had been successful for the decades prior to the flood.

Fast forward to 1995 after thousands of acres of private lands had been purchased and added to the Refuge. I felt it was time to make a complete review of the current hunt boundaries and factor in what new acreages needed to be brought in according to the promise we had made earlier. Sounds simple. Just the opposite, we were talking government here and a hunting community that was deeply invested emotionally in their sport. So, I decided to tread slowly and go about the decision using an Environmental Assessment (EA) format. Reason? The EA requires lots of public input and a thorough explanation behind your decision. The process is open to the public all the way.

So off we went on the process. I had lots of insight and opinion from Bob Ebeling and his numerous friends who were avid water-fowlers. That gave me a start. My personal hunting experiences on the Refuge also helped shape my judgment. Biologist Vicki Hirschboeck and I took the lead in contacting every group we knew about in addition to the "general public." We met with all the major hunt clubs and neighbors, requested input through advertisements and generally asked from input from wherever we could get it.

Then came the hard part, we had to succinctly write the pertinent information into a document that could be circulated to the public and provide alternatives for consideration. With lots of thought and staff time, we developed 5 alternatives for a new hunt plan and sent it out to everyone we could think of and asked for comments by a certain date. All 5 alternatives increased the hunt zone to satisfy the new expanded Refuge acreage, but each alternative had an emphasis. For example, one alternative opened more area accessible to airboats, while another opened more area suited to walk-in hunting. All 5 alternatives had unique advantages and disadvantages. But each alternative met strict biological scrutiny to manage migratory bird habitat and populations to meet Refuge objectives. That was where the bottom line had to be drawn. We truly wanted to provide an excellent hunt opportunity and, at the same time, provide excellent sanctuary for the birds. Not an easy balance to accomplish.

And boy did we get hit with the "lobbyists." It seemed like every organization sent a representative to make a pitch. That was ok, be-cause we wanted to have a full grasp of the issue from all viewpoints. I did not want any surprises due to ignorance on my part. When the dust settled, we had a stack of comments recommending their favorite alternative and why. We sorted the comments into the 5 alternatives and read through everyone. It came to decision time. What to do now? I relied back on my staff. I gave 5 staff an assignment to present or "sell" an alternative to staff at large. They were to present their best argument from reading all the comments and using any personal facts they wanted to add. So one fine morning the staff met for the 5 presentations and the entire staff then voted on paper for the one best alternative in their judgment. As it came out, one alternative came out way ahead--and luckily I agreed with it. That was that, and I made the decision to go with the alternative that is still in place today. It expanded the original 12,000 acres of huntable area up to nearly 18,000 acres, but most importantly, it increased the size of the sanctuary areas in Units 1 and 5. The 18,000 acres of hunt area included a great mix of delta, open water, grasslands and prairie wetlands. It was a decision I could justify with all groups, waterfowlers as well as birdwatchers-and I did many times. But most of all I was comfortable that the entire staff was involved and got to have a say in it, their buy-in was important to me.

In 1989, hunter use was very low. The lack of vegetation and vast expanse of either open water or mudflat was not conducive to hunting by the average hunter. A few hunters who were skilled with open water shooting faired ok in those years right after the flood, but they were the exception. The conditions changed rapidly in the early 1990's: Great Salt Lake receded quickly and fresh waters from the Bear River did their magic across the delta. Unit 1a and 2 were the first to sprout alkali bulrush, a prime marsh plant that attracted waterfowl and provided concealment for hunters. The Refuge attracted more waterfowl and hunters soon discovered that an excellent hunt could be had. Hunter success improved dramatically and so did the number of hunters. For unknown reasons another phenomenon was occurring, tundra swan use of the Refuge was increasing rapidly.

Before long, the Refuge became the place of choice for hunters with a "swan tag" to harvest their bird.

All that "good news" would normally be a recipe to declare success and feel good at the end of the day. But there is much more to this story. We had no law enforcement staff to oversee the hunt. As things got busy, some of the hunters began violating the regulations. It became too commonplace for some to shoot before and after legal hunting hours, go over the limit of ducks, hunt without "plugged" shotguns as well as fail to purchase a duck stamp. That kind of behavior catches on and increases as other hunters see violations going unenforced. Total enforcement personnel included myself, Claire Caldes (assistant manager) and Mark Laneer, but we were all certified officers who only did law enforcement as a collateral duty. That meant the Refuge had no full time officers to cover the 110 square mile area.

So, add up the mix of circumstances. More hunters, more waterfowl, swans on the increase, a hunt area that increased in size by 6,000 acres and very little law enforcement presence. That was a recipe for problems and it was not long before we were over our heads with bad-acting hunters. Nothing like trying to get a handle on hundreds of hunters on any one day spread out over thousands of acres. Well, a new "sheriff" was about to come to town and his name was Federal Agent Bob Standish.

Bob was hired to enforce wildlife laws over the Northern half of Utah. He was assigned to work anywhere there was a problem: on private, state or federal land. The agents usually spent most of their time off the Refuge because there were plenty of violations statewide. However, when Bob assisted us on the Refuge he was surprised at the number of violations he found. It was not long before he was spending a large portion of his time here and citing violations. To assist with the effort, I hired two temporary officers for the fall and they helped make a huge difference. Kelly Modla came on board first, then Rob

Hirschboeck and Dave Plank (replaced Kelly). At that point we were talking some serious officer power. This staff spent all day, every day on site. In 1996, there were 233 citations issued. In 1998 it had increased to 251. As word got out in successive years, compliance of regulations went way up and citation numbers declined accordingly.

One incident alone helped spread the word that Bob Standish meant business. Congress had declared that all refuges were to be closed temporarily because a federal budget had not been passed. We legally had no funds to operate the Refuge. I was instructed to post signs that the Refuge was closed to all public entry, which cut off all hunting. It was particularly irritating to waterfowl hunters because it was in the prime of fall migrations. It left a bitter taste, but the vast majority of law-abiding hunters accepted it for what it was--a political maneuver of party politics. One hunter, however, decided he "would not be kept out and entered a very remote area of the Refuge from waters of Bear River Bay. He set up decoys and made a hunt for the day, undetected. Or so he thought. He had a rotten attitude toward law enforcement, especially Federal law enforcement. In fact, he painted a NO FEDS sign on the rudder of his airboat for the world to see. His problem that day was that it was seen, albeit from a distance by Agent Bob Standish. Not being able to get access himself, Standish began his investigation as to who owned the "NO FEDS" airboat. When his investigation led him to the address, the resulting contact with the owner started to go ugly. The owner had a big attitude (surprise, surprise) and thought he was going to send Agent Standish packing due to lack of proof. Instead of leaving, Agent Standish backed his truck up to the airboat and hitched it on. The conversation immediately turned more "cooperative." A citation for hunting in a closed area was issued and payment was made. The world knew not to mess with Agent Standish. The goal in all this was not just to punish the violator: it was to bring the general hunting public into compliance with the regulations. The general level of compliance was definitely on its way up!

Since swan hunting was such a draw in the mid 1990's, some bad habits began to overshadow the hunt. One problem was "sky busting," a term used for blazing away at birds flying high up and out of effective shotgun range. This type of hunting commonly takes a place on a dike where swans will be flying over from their rest area. Each hunter takes numerous boxes of ammunition (25 shells per box) and hunkers down until the flocks of swans began to fly over. Instead of decoying a bird into close range, the sky buster simply shoots straight up in the air time after time, hoping for a lucky hit. Meanwhile lots of swans get hit with pellets that are not immediately lethal and they fly off wounded to die a slow death. Then every once in a while, swans do fall because so many shots are being fired. To make matters worse, a few trumpeter swans (rare, and largest swan in North America) are intermingled with the tundra swan flocks and cannot be identified to avoid being shot. This was causing, for good reason, the Trumpeter Swan Society to have a dim view of our hunt. I didn't like it either, so I became committed to eliminating the sky busting and raising the standard of the hunt. A good, ethical hunt should center around fair chase and a respect for the animal and its habitat. The swan hunt at Bear River Refuge had become the opposite. It had become a "shoot 'em up" contest with little regard for anything else.

Typically I dislike regulations, and I drag my feet when writing up new ones. However, this situation had become so bad I was ready to act in 1996. Writing up a new set of regulations is not that easy! After you put something on paper that sounds good, you have to read it from the standpoint of someone trying to take advantage or find a loophole. Wow. After taking way too much time and effort, I issued a number of regulations limiting swan hunters to only ten rounds of ammunition when they were in certain hunt areas. Other regulations were also issued to help improve the overall hunt quality. After an initial period of enforcement, the hunters as a whole came into line and we had a much better hunt.

Hunter access to the marsh was another issue that was addressed when the new hunt plan was enacted. Historically, access was quite limited. All hunters entered through the headquarters site and were checked in. Cars and trucks were parked there. Individuals gained access from there on foot (very difficult), small boat or via airboat within some areas. The basic public hunters without motorboats or airboats were really at a disadvantage, they just simply could not access very far into the wilds of the marshes. Former manager Ned Peabody tried to help the situation in the 1970's by building one parking lot on the northside of unit 2a. That helped some, but did not change the overall situation. I sought to make a major change. My rationale was that most hunters were average family people who held down jobs and had limited amounts of time and money. I wanted them to have a chance at good hunting without having to spend an entire day every time they wanted to go hunting. I hoped that the Refuge could provide day -long as well as half day hunts. To facilitate automobile access, the new plan allowed a number of smaller parking lots scattered around the perimeter of large hunt areas. More areas were also provided to launch boats. Great idea, right? An unforeseen problem developed with hunters jamming more cars into some of the areas than they were designed for and even parking up and down the dikes. Problem was, the access was becoming too liberal and hunters were crowding each other in some areas. We had to get a handle on this problem as well as the other problems that had developed with the hunt. So, sharp boundaries were posted for each parking lot and any car over the line was cited. Regulations also warned about staying inside the boundaries. Some hunters ignored the regulations and parked over the line. They got cited. Given some time with enforcement, a level of excellent compliance was achieved. Hunters became used to spreading out and giving each other the chance for a good hunt.

The long history of hunting on the Refuge is continuing. Today's acreage open to the public hunt is considerably larger than ever before and gives the "average hunter" a chance for excellent hunting throughout the season. The volunteers and local hunting public offered many good ideas while the new plan was developed.

All that effort means the tradition of waterfowl hunting will continue for another generation. The days afield with decoys, boats, dogs, calls and guns will bring young people and parents together in the arena of the marsh. By experiencing the untamed elements together, the bonds of family and friends are strengthened. The enjoyment, admiration and respect for nature runs deeper as well. It is my hope that the unique sights, sounds and fragrance of the fall marshes will forever be enjoyed by every Refuge visitor who chooses to participate in the full contact sport of hunting.

If you don't like the idea of shooting waterfowl, it is perfectly fine for you to cheer for the birds and hope the hunters shoot poorly. Truth is, a lot of older hunters are ok with coming home empty handed after a long day "away from it all" in the marsh. Looking back on my decades of waterfowl hunting, I never had a "bad" day no matter how the shooting went.

CHAPTER 22

PLAYING GOD, MANAGING WATER AND CREATING A LANDSCAPE

Shortly after applying for an expanded water right (see chapter 18), we had to justify the need for each acre/foot of water we requested. I would have preferred to just say we needed the whole Bear River flow forever and everyone else keep your hands off. Nice idea, but that does not hold up in court. There is a protocol of state law that must be addressed, as much as I hated that thought. I had always looked for the easy way out! Beyond legal reasons, it was also befitting the Refuge to take a much harder look at the way water was being managed and get the most out of this limited resource. In short, we needed a better planning process for water use, a proactive plan, not just one that amounted to flying by the seat of your pants day to day and running water wherever seemed best that day.

I was clueless where to start. Mind you, I LOVED going out all spring, summer and fall to divert water into the Refuge marsh units. It was such fun to just decide where to send water and "play God" by opening a water gate or pulling stoplogs to make it happen. It was fun alright, but not always the best way to make a decision. In fact, what usually SEEMED right at the time was not always the best decision in the long run. For years we had run the water management program in a free-wheeling sort of way. Maybe that is why it was so much fun; we just did what we wanted with no oversite or rigid process to follow. YIPPEE

Somehow, we had to quantify the river flows we needed throughout the year. The flow requirements had to be nailed down to reflect the birds' daily needs. In addition, flows for botulism control had to be justified in quantity and timing. Bob Green provided a key leadership role in this process. Although Bob was Chief of Water Resources in the Denver Regional Office, he was soon to retire and would give thousands of hours of volunteer expertise to this effort. I will report on that later.

The "kickoff" to this process was a closed door meeting with a group of local bird experts. Some of the members where from Utah Division of Wildlife Resources, Utah State University and several non-profit organizations (Audubon, Friends of Great Salt Lake, etc.). I invited the most knowledgeable and experienced people available. The group was asked to list all the bird species utilizing the Refuge and what they were doing (resting, feeding, nesting, etc.) on January 1 of each year. Then the same question was repeated for EACH DAY OF THE YEAR. That's right, every day of a typical year was discussed for bird use. For me, it was fun just to hear the experts discuss their collective insights and knowledge.

From the information of daily bird use, the next step was asking the experts what specific kind of habitat it would take to fulfill the daily needs. A description of those habitats became a daily portrait of how the Refuge wetlands needed to look over the course of the year. That portrait became the habitat plan and it contained 12 distinct wetland types. How is that for specific? Acreages for each habitat type were quantified. Finally, water requirements were calculated for each habitat type on a daily basis throughout the year. Water needs to flush the marshes during botulism outbreaks was added and the grand total was our water right filing. It was a big number – nearly one third of the total annual river flow, but we felt it could be justified in court if necessary.

First, it had to be accepted by the Utah Division of Water Rights. The director was Bob Morgan, a well-respected leader by most of us in the field. He had to justify his decisions to the governor as well as local people. There was a balance he had to maintain between conservation and other uses. Not an easy job. When Bob looked over our justification for the Refuge water filing, he accepted our numbers and I was elated. We could, in fact, move ahead with our plans and hope to get a "certificated "water right for the amount we justified.

Getting down to specifics on how to best use our water resources was put on paper beginning in 1997 with a Comprehensive Management Plan (CMP). There was lots of very tedious paperwork here, done mostly by biologist Vicki Hirschboeck. Since I hate planning (even though I realize it is necessary), it seemed like an overwhelming process. As soon as Vicki's CMP was done, we went right into a number of "step-down" plans. They included plans to control predators (controversial), manage upland habitats, manage water, control noxious weeds and monitor our management actions.

We developed a kind of personality balance in the office between Vicki and me. I was the guy who was wanting to be doing something all the time. It didn't matter what, just do something. It could be shoot all the foxes and raccoons one day and spray all the salt cedar trees the next. Let's build a new dike, put in another water control structure.......Well you get the idea. Do now, plan later. Vicki was much better at making sure we were doing things that fit into a larger scientific grid. In other words, she wanted to make sure our actions made scientific sense! She was quite vocal when I got too pushy with something that was not analyzed properly. So, we hit a good balance – I pushed and dreamed daily, but she moderated with intelligence. We got along great and appreciated each other's personality.

It was determined we needed two comprehensive plans: A water management plan and a habitat management plan. These two plans would provide the long term guidance and approvals to do the best job with our lands, water, and wildlife. Vicki went to work and designed a study in cooperation with Utah State University in 1999 to measure nest success and how it was affected by grazing on our newly purchased grasslands (the Grassland Habitat Unit). Also, in the same year Vicki helped design a research project on mammalian predators--raccoons, skunk and fox-- to determine their home range and movements as well as their affects on nesting. Both studies led to Doctorate degrees for Ben West and Nicki Frey.

When the research project on mammalian predators was completed, it led to finishing a Predator Management Plan. Basically, we got the go ahead to officially kill predators that had reduced our nest success to only 6%. When control measures were instituted, nesting success immediately jumped to over 50%. That was real success.

Secondly, the grassland research project revealed that the winter grazing program we used to enhance the health of prairie grasses did no harm to spring nesting birds. That good news gave us the go-ahead to manage grasslands with winter cattle grazing. Winter grazing was the easiest and most cost effective way for us to maintain healthy grasslands.

After receiving excellent reviews from our Regional Office and other peers, Vicki and her biological trainee Karen Lindsay were asked to be contributors in a national Shorebird Management Plan, specifically to describe how Great Salt Lake fits into the international picture.

The crowning achievement in management planning was accomplished by another biologist, Bridget Olson, who arrived on duty in

2002. The requirements for a nationally approved Habitat Management Plan had been revised and had a whole new level of required detail. WORK, WORK, WORK. In my career, plans were required for just about everything and I had a basic policy. That was, just crank something out that gives the minimum and get back to real work as soon as possible. This plan, however, was the one exception.

Bridget took the biological information that was amassed from our earlier effort on bird use and daily wetland requirements. She "married" wetland requirements to daily water needs PER WETLAND UNIT (about 30 all together) and then used the current year river flow forecast to predict what flows of water we could plan to receive. Then, having a good idea of flows the river would deliver in spring, summer and fall, the staff could develop a priority list of units to fill. That was where the rubber met the road. The Refuge could begin the water year in late winter with a year long plan on what units to fill and maintain. That had never been done. For once, the Refuge had a Wetland Habitat "Business Plan." We put it on-line so the general public could see why water was going to any specific area (or not). When we submitted the plan for Regional and Washington review, it was the first and only approved plan of its kind. It would serve as a national model in the following years. And one more thing. It was not a typical plan that was put on a shelf and never taken off; it was useful in the field and office as well. We referred to it frequently--the biggest compliment you can pay a plan. In addition, the plan also applied to the Grassland Habitat Unit (refer to Chapter 25).

As for "milk toast biologists" you may encounter them from place to place, but the Bear River Refuge biologists were far from that. My highest respect goes to Vicki, Bridget and Karen for showing the grit to finish a long term job in excellent fashion. They made me look good, even though it was their project from start to finish..

CHAPTER 23

SPECIAL APPROPRIATIONS, FINISHING THE HABITAT WORK

In 1989, floodwaters were withdrawing and the full magnitude of devastation was brought to light. All bridges, dikes, buildings, water control structures and everything above ground was completely leveled. It was evident that the entire Refuge would need to be rebuilt.

As described earlier, the corps of volunteers began work soon after I arrived under the supervision of Bob Ebeling. They immediately began the long road of restoring the Refuge to its former glory. They took on some huge jobs like resetting the concrete bridge decks across the mouth of the river. Dozens of water control structures were refitted with flashboards, catwalks and guard rails. Dikes were repaired enough to impound water as early as spring of 1990. Gravel was spread and access around Unit 2 and along D line was restored. An unbelievable accomplishment by volunteers supervising themselves with no federal funding and having to raise all their monies for materials through private donations.

So, what to do. In 1989 I was totally new, and inexperienced, in working with a volunteer staff and even worse I was totally in the dark about working with the Washington D.C. budgeting process to get the necessary funds. My career experience was totally on refuges in the Dakotas and Nebraska. The only influence I knew how to make on the Refuge budget was to inform my supervisor of the needs we had and hope to high heaven that he sent it on up the ladder to people who could (and would) help. As I was to discover, that approach is tantamount to failure. I just did not know any better. Short of divine intervention, I was on a trajectory of failure.

Then came the right people at just the right time, even before I knew how badly I needed them. Call it extreme luck time and time again, or call it what I do – divine intervention.

Meeting Bob Valentine in August of 1989 was the first major milestone. He said, "Let me know if you need any help," My initial reaction was that since I needed federal money and he was with Box Elder County he would not have enough influence to do me any good. When he offered to get an "add on" of $50,000 in the current year's budget, I said, "Sure go ahead." Deep inside I was skeptical because I had never heard of such a thing happening to a refuge. Surprising me, and my supervisor, the funding was added to my budget several weeks later. It came directly from Washington and "earmarked" for Bear River Refuge. Wow. More about Valentine and his contacts later.

The next "lucky" connection came when Lee Baxter, a Bureau of Reclamation employee, called me to ask if he could help under a cooperative agreement recently signed between the Bureau and the Fish and Wildlife Service. He offered to come up from Provo and look over the Refuge with me to see if he could figure out a way to get us some assistance from the Bureau. I was skeptical that anything would really come from the gesture, but I was willing to invest a day of my time. Lee struck me as a highly capable employee right away. Initially, he offered up some engineering services from the Provo office and it seemed that may be of some value. But still, what do you do with engineering services when you are too broke to build anything?

The big break came when Lee informed me that a "drought relief" program was approved by Congress for this area and he would be willing to apply for $500,000 for Refuge work. Had it not been for Lee suggesting the $500,000, I probably would have asked for much less. Well, the proposal was approved and we were into the first "big money" of the restoration. As we were in the middle of some dike restoration in Unit 3, Lee informed me that another program was approved, this time for flood relief. Well, we got approved for that too and melded the money together to finish the dike work in addition to other projects. It was humorous (if not a little gray) that we put drought and flood relief money together on a single project! Glad nobody noticed – and, the statute of limitations is over.

Next, my good friend Bob Valentine was appointed as a commissioner on the "URMCC," an acronym for Utah Reclamation Mitigation Conservation Commission. Wew, lucky I can still remember all that. It amounts to a funding arm of the Central Utah Project to mitigate for environmental impacts that were made during construction of water development features in Utah. Bob coordinated with me to fund the purchase of some major water management facilities that we installed on the Refuge. It was worth hundreds of thousands and amounted to another big boost.

Still, the Fish and Wildlife Service was unable to tap into a sizable funding source for Bear River. Had we been depending on them for securing funds for us, we would still be accomplishing next to nothing at this point.

Then, the Bob Valentine/Jim Hansen connection kicked into gear and over an eleven year period, starting in Fiscal year 91, Bear River received "earmarked" construction money annually to complete restoration work on the original network of dikes and water control structures PLUS the construction of an additional 50 miles of new dikes and 50 water control structures. These new dikes would create more management units that would improve the quality of wildlife habitat and better utilize water.

Due to strict regulations, as a government employee I was not allowed to lobby for money. Budget requests were made by our office in Washington D.C. through well defined channels. So, Bob Valentine did all the "requesting" for me and kept me out of trouble. I just met with Bob and told him what I would need to keep the restoration going. He would talk to Jim Hansen and presto, like magic, it would show up as construction funding in my budget. I don't know of another refuge that had anything like that kind of pipeline. It really kept us moving ahead with our work and not having to worry about the annual whims of the administration. And yes, once in a while I received comments from other refuges who had almost nothing (they had to think twice about even buying a pair of hip boots). And no, I never took the goodwill of Bob Valentine for granted. I knew I was the luckiest "kid" in the Region.

Over the twelve years, total funds for construction were $3.2 million. If you are used to dealing with highway projects or defense contracts, that kind of money is next to nothing, but to the Refuge it was HUGE. That enabled us to pay wages for two temporary, full time equipment operators (Doug Hadley and Rod Jacobson) as well as purchase fuel, rip/rap, gravel, concrete, steel, culverts...., well, you get the idea. Those funds went straight to "moving dirt" and building water control structures. We were on very friendly terms with Congressman Hansen and his staff. Whenever possible, we gave tours to show off what we had done with the special funds. Those were fun tours and I was very proud of the accomplishments the staff and volunteers had made. I was told by Hansen's staff, "Nobody stretches the dollars like you guys do." That was the ultimate compliment to a maintenance staff who took their work seriously and did the very best they could. We all did our level best to make sure that would remain the case.

CHAPTER 24

"JUST GET 'ER DONE," THE IWANSKI LEGACY

Upon my arrival to the Refuge in August of 1989, no other employees were there to join me. I worked "alone" with the corps of volunteers until I was able to hire a clerk to help with office paperwork a few months later. If you have ever run a field office, the Clerk is an essential position. I won't bother you with details here, but he or she does all the paperwork to keep your paycheck coming on time, plus a hundred other things that have to be done to keep the office afloat.

The next position came in the late summer of 1990, when I was able to fill the position of Assistant Manager – or Deputy. I selected Claire Caldes for that position and she fit right in immediately. She wound up staying over 10 years, but that is another story in itself. Claire was energetic and worked well with the volunteers and took on any job I gave her. Our biggest need at that point was to have a maintenance employee who could tackle the mammoth job of restoring the physical damage to the Refuge. This was not the job for anyone of average or even typical skills and drive. We were looking for a very special kind of person when we advertised for the position. We needed a "ramrod" kind of employee who would take a job and run with it.

Sifting through the applications, we eventually zeroed in on the paperwork from Rich Iwanski. He was stationed at Crescent Lake Refuge, in the western sandhills of Nebraska. Crescent Lake Refuge is extremely remote and a difficult place for families with young children. The "public school" was still a one room rural school with only a few kids in grades 1-6. Likewise, the Refuge work required dedication and an element of ingenuity because you could not run to town when you needed something or get a service call from the local implement dealer. The Refuge staff lived on site and traveled dirt roads for miles when headed for town, which wasn't very often.

After a glowing report from his supervisor, we hired Rich without meeting him in person. Unfortunately, that is common practice for our organization. Money was not "wasted" on paying travel expenses to meet job applicants. Rich's boss was Kevin Brenin, a fellow refuge manager that I had known for decades. I relied on my friendship with Kevin to get the "low down" on Rich" I really did not care how good the application looked. My question to Kevin was straight on: "Was he any good," I asked, and "should I hire him?" This is where refuge managers were straight with each other. Kevin knew I would never forgive him if he "oversold" Rich. I needed the truth. Was he great, good or just fair?

"When you give him a job, he does it right every time," Kevin said. "It was 30 degrees below zero one winter morning with a stiff north wind. At first light I heard a truck fire up and Rich was already headed out to fill pheasant feeders. It was a Saturday." Bingo. That was the kind of employee I was looking for. We called Rich and offered him the job.

We had no way of knowing, but we had just hired the best person possible for the challenges we faced. God was sending us the one person who was perfectly suited to get the job done. Beyond having a personal interest in the Refuge, Rich was a self starter on the job.

He had the qualities of being a visionary, so he could see the possibilities of the future. His other strong sides were creativity, pride in workmanship and efficiency (faster, better and cheaper). When we planned to do a project, I could depend on his construction estimates to be right on. There always comes a time when the plans are done and work starts. Rich turned into a driving force to get it done right and get it done as quickly as possible. The special construction funding we received directly from Congress (not through our agency) was directly attributed to his planning, oversite and drive to see each project through. Congressional staff were more than impressed by the work he accomplished with the funds they secured for each step of the restoration. Every time we got a special appropriation, Rich used it well and we got more. That's how it worked.

Early on I had an agreement with Rich: When we were inside the office I was "in charge," when we were outside on the job he was "in charge." That agreement served us well over the next 15 years. I also discovered another trait about Rich. When we talked over a job and came to an agreement as to what was needed and how the finished product would function, Rich would invariably take my ideas and come up with a better finished product than I expected. He loved surprising me by doing better than expected. I loved it too.

When Rich arrived, we only had a rented shop building in the abandoned "Indian School" property. Our main office was off Main Street in a strip mall next door to a pizza restaurant. We had no equipment and very few tools and supplies. It was a bit of a let-down for Rich, coming from Crescent Lake where they at least had acquired a few pieces of heavy equipment. I was "betting on the come" and had my fingers crossed that somehow we would get enough funding to keep a man like him busy doing something good.

His level of dedication to the job first showed up when a herd of trespass cattle crossed the Refuge boundary in Units 5&6 because the boundary fence had been taken out by the flood. We had miles of fence to construct to protect the Refuge from the daily damage the cattle were doing. Coming from a farm and working in the sandhills of Nebraska, this was right up Rich's alley. We purchased fence posts, wire and an electric charger. Rich went right to work--by himself. In short order he had placed all the posts and strung all the wire. When he hooked up the charger, the fence was complete and did its job. As a side note, the boundary--about 5 miles--was devoid of survey pins. Rich had to determine a straight line by eyeballing back on a couple of witness posts he had driven, hardly a method to be recommended for accuracy. At the time, I felt the fence was surely off the legal line but could be corrected later. I just wanted a fence to keep the cattle out. Years later our Regional Surveyors verified Rich's eyeballed fence as right on. He had carried a straight line for three miles out across a mudflat. I was totally shocked. Rich was not surprised at all: he had confidence in his "eyeballing."

We began to pick up equipment one piece at a time from some of the special funds we received. We got a backhoe first, then used some of the drought relief money (from Bureau of Reclamation) to purchase a tractor. Money from another project helped buy a tracked backhoe. As we progressed into more and more projects involving excavation and construction, we built the heavy equipment inventory piece by piece. The magic ingredient here is that we would have a job approved with oversite by the Engineering Division in the Regional Office. Once they gave approval (which was every time), we had a set amount of money we could use for the job. The amount of funding for each project was based on a national standard of what the project should cost. So, each time we took the money, there was enough for us to buy a piece of equipment as well as all the materials we needed to finish the job. Presto, we had a new piece of equipment when the job was over--all because we did the job below estimates. Sweet deal. It worked every time. As time went on, Rich and the crew got even more efficient. For example, the upgrade of structures in Whistler Canal were completed for less than ten percent of the engineering estimate! All the "extra money" was used for a BIG PARTY. No, just kidding. More supplies were purchased for doing other "bonus" projects to show Congress. We partied on our own dimes.

Soon after Rich came on board, we were able to add Tim Woodward, an experienced equipment operator, to our staff. By this time we had some equipment and planned on keeping him busy in the field all year with building dikes and other heavy construction duties. As we demonstrated our ability to get the job done, Bob Valentine and Jim Hansen kept our annual construction funds coming. Another heavy equipment operator, Doug Hadldey, was hired later on to join the crew. He was hired under a term appointment which meant he could work as long as our special appropriations came. By the same token, he would have to be let go if and when the special funds dried up. Hiring Rod Jacobson in 1998 rounded out the maintenance/construction crew to four employees. He came with a background in construction, which was a valuable asset when coupled with his work ethic. They made a great team out there on the ground tackling any job we had. Rich, of course, was their supervisor and planned the daily work along with all supplies and equipment needed. The accomplishments of this team became noticed not only in our Denver Regional Office, but in Washington as well.

Our annual tours for Congressional staff were a highlight. It was my pleasure, more like my pride and joy, to show off the construction accomplishments each year. It amounted to a full day on the Refuge-- not hard when you have 110 square miles of property. We would travel dikes in various stages of completion. That means we ventured over some dikes for miles that were just mounds of dirt piled high. Other sections were leveled and graded but had no gravel. This always made for an "adventurous" trip. More than once, we got stuck in the mud and had to radio for help to get out. We also had airboat rides as part of the tours. The airboat gave the Congressional people a unique look at the marshes and some of the dike rehab. But really, it was a huge amount of fun! Those folks were locked inside offices most of the time and when we jumped into an airboat and flew across the shallows of the Refuge, it was a highlight. And here is another little secret, I let them drive the airboat when we were in the middle of nowhere. They loved the experience and I think it helped them appreciate the Refuge in a personal way. That kind of experience is more valuable than a thousand slide shows or presentations. All this is to say that my pride in the Refuge was possible because of the constant progress that Rich and the crew made. I like to think my pride in the work rubbed off on the decision makers as they saw the accomplishments for themselves.

While the paid staff were accomplishing project after project, the volunteers were also doing their part. After we got into full construction mode in the mid 1990's, the volunteers took up more of a supporting role. They stayed active with building public use facilities like wooden platforms for overlooking the marshes, placing signs along the Unit 2 auto tour route, helping deliver supplies and a thousand other duties that saved other employees time and effort. The presence of the volunteers, along with their encouragement, remained a central part of the Refuge "culture" throughout my tenure at the Refuge. I will say it again and again: "We would not have restored the Refuge in my lifetime if there were no volunteers. They struck the spark and set the pace early on. My truly EXCEPTIONAL staff carried the ball from there. I was blessed by being in the middle of an exceptional team doing their magic."

All tolled, our special construction funding from Congress came over a 12 year period and amounted to $3.2 million-- or an average of $267,000 per year. Not a huge sum at all if you happen to work for another agency that goes through the big bucks. But for a refuge, that is a windfall beyond dreams. If spent carefully, that will purchase concrete, gravel, fuel, repair equipment and pay overtime. It gave our four man team the ability to work their hearts out and get the job done.

I do need to point out that we did receive $150,000 total in that same time period from regular funding channels for construction. I don't want to sound like a spoiled child. I was glad to get it, but it definitely was much less than what our Congressional offices produced.

In 1998, work was focused to finish the sub--dividing of Unit 3. Way back before the flood, plans were made to subdivide this unit into smaller, more manageable, sub-units. With smaller units, water could be applied more precisely to grow better food and cover plants as well as control carp. We planned even more sub--units after the flood in our master plan. We were keen on getting this unit complete and in operation so we could show off the benefits first hand. To that end, our crew spread 66 tons of crushed rock to riprap dike slopes and covered the roadway with 25,000 cubic yards of gravel. A total of 9 water control structures were built to control inflows and outflows to impoundments. For vehicle travel over bridge decks, 750 feet of guard rails were installed. Rubble from the ruins of the "Duckville Clubhouse" was removed. To subdivide Unit 5, another 2 miles of dikes were completed at the same time. And finally (wew), improvements were made on water sources in the Grassland Habitat Unit.

Rich's creativity was put to work when we were considering how to build the dozens of new water control structures needed for each subdivided unit. These concrete structures are placed through the dikes to direct the flow of water downstream and hold a specific depth in the pond above. A concrete deck with guardrail serves as a bridge for vehicles driving along the dike. The original structures were built "in place" by excavating enough dirt to build foundations for concrete floors and walls. This was a slow and expensive process. Rich gave it some thought and designed a similar structure that was built by assembling a number of pre-cast concrete parts. Rich's design was stronger, cheaper and faster to install. A big win from all angles. To present his idea to our Regional Engineers, Rich built a wooden model with all the component parts cut to scale. With Engineering approval, the design went to our Division of Contracting so they could request formal bids. We awarded the bid to Colorado Precast Company and later received a stockpile of unassembled concrete parts which we stored on the Refuge for use as needed. This single "invention" alone will put Rich on the permanent superstar list, saving hundreds of thousands over the years.

In 1999, Bob Valentine gave the Refuge yet another boost from his position as a director on the URMCC. This federal agency was set up to provide wetland mitigation for the Central Utah Project (a water development project). He championed our cause and we received funding for 7 large concrete water control structures to be placed in "D" line as well as another 20,000 tons of crushed rock for graveling dikes. In addition, the Whistler 3-Way structure was rehabilitated and nine miles of dikes were given the finishing slopes and road surface. The crew was truly into full stride!

Just in case you are thinking that the staff had too much time on their hands in 1999, I also need to say that the shop building was also constructed that year. The 15,900 square foot building was contracted out to Furst Construction, but I wanted our staff to do all of the excavation and foundation work to bring down costs. Furst Construction was reluctant and replied that they only hired "the best," insinuating my crew would not be up to their standards. I promised that we would meet their specifications on time AND that without our guys doing the excavation and foundations there would be no contract with Furst. When the building was complete and we finished inspection, the supervisor from Furst Construction said, "You have the best working for you." Proudly, I agreed!

When planning for the work season of 2000, it was evident we needed more equipment operators to get the job done. Steve Hicks joined the staff that year, filling the vacancy left by Claire Caldes when she accepted a position in Alaska. Steve was another "get the job done" kind of guy who knew his way around equipment and construction. I put word out that we needed a good operator willing to come to Bear River on temporary duty for the summer and work long hours. Offering overtime pay is a big carrot in our outfit because it rarely happens and some employees jump at the rare chance of having a larger paycheck once in a while. Madison Wetland District in South Dakota responded. Their maintenance man, Earl Kuaker was willing to come. Earl had left a good reputation with Steve (not easy to get), and so I approved Earl's temporary transfer to Bear River for the month of August.

With cooperation from the weather, construction in 2000 started in April and went through October. Work zeroed in on dikes subdividing Unit 3 and Unit 4 as well as O Line canal. In addition to dike construction, concrete water control structures were installed from O Line canal into Units 3G, 3F, 3E and 4A. A drain canal was also started in Unit 4 as well as topping many miles of dike roads with rock and steel mill slag aggregate. Use of the slag was Rich's idea. This material is cheaper than gravel and works just as well.

We became wary of contract dirt work in the early years of the restoration because it was a struggle to get contractors mobilized when soil conditions were right. Depending on the site, soils may only be dry for a few weeks each year in late summer/early fall. Missing that window means the work does not get done. Riding herd on contractors is time consuming and frustrating. Of course, most contractors are out to do the minimum amount of work with the lowest passing quality. Sorry to those of you who are good contractors, but that was our experience. After several bad experiences, we decided that doing it ourselves was cheaper and resulted in a better product. Wow, those would be fighting words to my private contractor dad! I want to bring out one exception of contract work we were totally happy with, Buttars Construction. They secured a contract to build O Line canal. Those guys showed up on time with the right equipment and worked 24 hours/day for 90 days to complete the work. They did not pull off site until the job was completely finished. Major kudos, and a tip of my hat for that company.

About that same time, Rich learned how to "milk" another source of money. Each refuge could apply for money under a source named "Maintenance Management System" or MMS. The process called for estimating the total cost of your project according to a standardized list of costs. If approved, that amount of money was moved into your refuge budget. CH CHING .. Now comes the good part. We took that money and instead of putting the project out to private contract (expensive), we kept the money and did the work ourselves. We used the money to buy all the supplies and pay the wages of employees to do the work. Then, we KEPT THE REST. We used this windfall to stockpile supplies to do even more work. During inspections, I was forthright about what we did and showed the results of doing more than expected. Definitely operating in the "gray zone," but doing it for a good reason. In 2000, the "standard estimated" cost of building a retaining wall on the riverbank near headquarters was $160,000. Remember that was using THEIR numbers and it was supposed to reflect a fair private contract cost. Rich and his crew said they would do the work, so we kept the funds and completed the work for only $40,000. We used the "windfall" to purchase rip/rap for use on some dikes that had erosion issues. Is that pimping the system? I loved improving the Refuge budget that way. So did Rich.

Lots of refuges did not jump in on this process. Sorry to say, not every staff wanted to take on extra work, save money and then get more done. Iwanski and his team were only too anxious to take on whatever they had to. And of course, that made me look good.

When 2001 rolled around, it became the "big year of dirt work." The staff were hitting their stride. There was lots of work to do and the resources were lined up ahead to just go for it. A total 580,000 cubic yards of dirt was moved to construct dikes, canals and nesting islands. Rich's precast water control structures were installed in cross dikes. The south structure in Whistler 3-way was rebuilt. Once again, we advertised for help from other refuge equipment operators. The deal included unlimited work and unlimited overtime. That was music to good equipment operators. They were given a machine and a job excavating that stretched to the horizon. We had staff from 10 refuges come for the work. We took a $500,000 appropriation and rented heavy equipment, bought fuel and paid wages. YEEE HAWW. The Refuge was a beehive and we ripped it up. Work was completed on Unit 4 and then on Unit 2D. All told, 7.2 miles of dike were built and another 6.25 were surfaced with rock and road base gravel. Unit 4 was completed in time to refill when the river flows came back in the fall. The entire project fell on Rich Iwnaski's shoulders for planning and executing.

Listed below are specific projects completed that year by this dedicated crew. The list is impressive, but seeing it on the ground was even better.

* Finished sloping O-Line east side with dozer
* Formed in place the south 4-bay structure on the Whistler 3-way
* Built and sloped the west dike of Whistler bypass on east side of Unit 4c

* Built, sloped and rip/rapped four nesting islands—two in Unit 4c and two in Unit 4b
* Built and sloped lateral dikes on the north side of Unit 4b and 4c
* Placed rock on top of half the length of the cross dike between Units 3f and 3g
* Placed rock and road base on the east side of O-Line and half of the west side
* Placed rock on half the length of 4b lateral
* Placed dirt fill for Unit 2d cross dike and completed half of the sloping and leveling
* Formed concrete in place for flap-gate inlets into Units 3a1, 3a2 and 3h
* Formed concrete in place for outlet structure in Unit 3d
* Installed precast inlet water control structure in Unit 4b
* Formed concrete in place for boat ramp at historic headquarters site

I doubt if there will ever be another year like that unless millions of $$ are appropriated and an army of people are employed. All of this was done "in house" with a relatively small amount of funding. It was kept simple and closely supervised at the field level. No funds were sucked off by Regional Engineering and Contracting (up to 35% if they get involved).

In 2002 work was focused on one last cross dike in Unit 2. This is a dike that sectioned off the northwest corner of Unit 2, creating a sub-unit labeled 2C. When the dirt work was completed, steel mill aggregate was placed on the surface. While that major project was being completed, two nesting islands were built in Unit 4. Since the O line canal was completed, a concrete inlet structure had to be built where it joined the Bear River channel. This large structure was designed by

Rich to hold two 16 foot steel radial gates and had to be constructed in place with formed concrete. Spanning several seasons, this project enabled up to 1,000 cubic feet per second to be diverted off the Bear River to bypass floodwaters and also supply parts of Unit 4 and Unit 3 with water.

Rich, Tim, Rod and Doug by no means rested on their laurels after that banner year. They continued being productive and dedicated right through the restoration (2006). Their day to day accomplishments energized me and I felt a sense of responsibility to fulfill my duties to a higher standard as well. I can't honestly say I matched their level.

CHAPTER 25

THE GRASSLAND UNIT, A NEW TYPE OF HABITAT

The "original" Refuge boundaries established in 1928 included 64,500 acres. The vast majority of this area was marsh with very few acres of grassy uplands included. Through the ensuing decades, biological evaluations noted that the lack of uplands were a limitation to the success of the numerous species of ground nesting birds. However, no acquisition of surrounding upland habitat was accomplished. In 1983-89, the floodwaters brought a halt to normal Refuge operations and provided the crisis needed to focus on the future. In some ways, the flood was a blessing. It forced us to take a hard look at what the Refuge needed to be productive into the long term future.

I led the process of standing back and looking at over 50 years of Refuge history and proposing a plan for the future. It was a lot of fun! My boss, Barney Schranck, gave me free rein in developing the plan. In addition to going through all the information in historic files and reports, I "hit the street" to talk to everyone who had experience or knowledge of the Refuge. It was interesting to gain the perspective of Refuge employees spanning previous decades. Other sources were college professors like John Kadlec and Jess Low. Managers from the neighboring Utah Waterfowl Management Areas (Salt Creek and

Ogden Bay) were valuable in giving me insight. I even spent time talking to neighboring farmer/ranchers. They had perspectives that needed to be considered. Talking to the "general public" gave me the opinions of hunters, birdwatchers, sight seers and the myriad of people who used the Refuge in different ways. Not to be forgotten are the Utah Department of Natural Resources personnel, especially those involved with Water Rights (Bob Morgan and Bob Fotheringham). The neighboring waterfowl hunt clubs were also important contributors to the "information bank." Among the largest were the Canadian Goose Club, Bear River Club, Chesapeake Club, Davis Club, Pintail Club and Premium Club. Sounds impressive, but remember I was the new kid on the block and had zero knowledge about the history and needs of this area that resembled a moonscape at that time.

What came through loud and clear was that the Refuge was sorely lacking in grassy uplands. These habitats are favored areas for many birds throughout the seasons. Most notably, several species of ducks and geese utilize grasslands for nesting. In addition, white-faced ibis and sandhill cranes use grassy meadows for feeding and resting.

So the time came to take out a map of the area and draw a line that I could defend as the expansion plan for the Refuge. Remember, everything I was about to propose was privately owned land. In case you forgot, Utah is already 80% Federal land. Every acre I proposed for purchase would be taking it out of private land and into Federal ownership. You get the idea; this was a touchy issue. Going for everything might not be practical if the local folks objected. Going for too little would not get the Refuge what it needed.

I decided to go ahead with an aggressive proposal, sort of a go-for-broke approach. I circled a proposed acquisition boundary that totaled 40,000 acres. Was I nuts or what? The 40,000 acres was made up of a 22,000 acre proposal for wetland easements and 18,000 for actual fee title purchase. The new boundary brought the east side of the Refuge all the way out to Interstate 15 and encompassed a grassy upland area that was being utilized for grazing and haying. It was the perfect grassland habitat that the Refuge was lacking.

As I described earlier, this acquisition proposal would not have been approved had it not been for the Friends of Bear River, specifically Bob Valentine. Bob had ties with Governor Norm Bangerter and convinced him to approve my plans. That made it an "official" acquisition plan and we were able to go out and purchase land inside that boundary line. And purchase we did.

The initial purchase started quite to my surprise one morning when an elderly man was waiting at my office door before I arrived. He introduced himself as Winn Nichols and said he had some land that the Refuge should buy. Ooookkkkk. I jumped into his rig and we took a ride out West Forest street until we arrived at his 1,122 acre property. It was within our acquisition boundary – check. It was the kind of habitat we were looking for – check. He was a willing seller – check.

I returned to the office and called Paul Hartman, the Chief of Realty in the Regional Office. It took some doing, but Paul initiated the land acquisition process and we eventually closed on the property for $340 per acre! After that first land purchase, I contacted other landowners within our approved acquisition area and eventually added a total of 8,348 acres to the Refuge by 1997.

That process was so enjoyable. It amounted to looking up landowners and sitting down in their home to discuss the sale of their land. With some landowners, they immediately showed an interest in selling and it was as easy as shaking hands and explaining how an appraiser would determine fair market value and then they would be given an offer on paper. Other landowners needed to think about it for a while before deciding to sell. Once in a while, a landowner would just say "No thanks." Either way, I tried to remain on friendly terms in

case landowners changed their minds (that happened occasionally after the death of a family member). One landowner sold to the Refuge
because he did NOT want the area to eventually be sold to his neighbors – he was over 90 years old. Other landowners sold because they
did not want their land to be developed. Some just wanted a fair price
and a quick source of cash.

With the new purchases came the responsibility to manage the
lands for their greatest productivity. That meant fencing the boundaries, putting up Refuge signs, cleaning up junk piles and maintaining/
improving irrigation systems. Refuge volunteers, especially Norm
Layton loved spending time with me and other employees fixing fence
and posting new boundaries. Norm and other volunteers also cleaned
up litter and trash from years of neglect. Volunteers also helped with
managing irrigation water--something that turned out to be a bigger
job than any of us anticipated.

Another one of those "God moments" was happening before I recognized it. This time it came in the form of a phone call from a retired
Denver Regional Office employee, Bob Green. I knew Bob well because he had worked on water rights issues during the intense months
following the Federal Reserved Water Right filing (see chapter 18).
Bob served as Chief of Water Rights for a number of years and was
very highly respected for his knowledge and experience. Bob told me
on the phone that he wanted to be a volunteer! He was self contained
in a travel trailer and willing to set up house keeping in Brigham City
for an extended period and give us a hand. I was elated, knowing we
had a lot for Bob to do. But truthfully, I had no idea how much I needed him. There was a "grundle" of water rights with the new lands we
had purchased and I was WAY underestimating the work it was going
to take to get it all straightened out. Ignorance was bliss in my case.

Over the span of a few years we had acquired 22 separate water rights "attached" to the land we had purchased. It summed up to

54,000 acre/feet of water annually! That is a lot of water, enough to cover 84 square miles with a foot of water. We had numerous details to settle with water turns, splitting up water sources with other land-owners, improving delivery facilities and other details. Solving those issues would take a lawyer and someone who knew the ins and outs of water management. Bob was uniquely qualified in both arenas. Imagine how much of a blessing this was for me. A volunteer arrives who can serve as my Philadelphia lawyer, surveyor, title inspector, project planner, design engineer, water expert, contracting special-ist and personal mentor. That's right, I came to cherish Bob's advice on a wide range of issues that crossed my desk on a daily basis. His advice and guidance was full of wisdom and experience. He helped me through a lot of decisions that I was grappling with. It is not an exaggeration to say he never let me down.

Bob went right to work and became as productive, and even more so, than a full time paid staff. Digging right into the recorded wa-ter rights, Bob began the long process of organizing and quantify-ing each water right. He accessed the state data base and additional information on each and every deed. From my staff, I had assigned Joe Saenz, an inexperienced Trainee to oversee the new acquisitions. I would have preferred someone with a lot of experience, but our staff was still small and we all had more than a full time job on our plates. That meant I expected everyone to "rise to the need." I knew Joe was overwhelmed, but there was not a whole lot I could do about it. So was everyone else on staff.

Bob came to the rescue. He "buddied up" with Joe right away and gave him an unlimited source of personal mentoring into the world of water rights. What an opportunity for the Refuge. What an opportu-nity for me. And especially, what an opportunity for Joe!

First thing, Bob looked at the new area – its vegetation and water resources--and coined the title "Grassland Habitat Unit." That title stuck permanently. We began to look at this block of land as a separate unit that was to be managed separately, but in coordination with the "original Refuge" which was mainly marshlands of various sorts.

That first year, 1996, Bob served 206 volunteer hours. WOW, and that was just the first installment of what was to become his long term commitment to the Refuge. He followed up in 1997 with 600 hours and in 1998 with 322 hours. Continuing in 1999 and 2000 he served 608 and 684 respectively. He returned each spring through 2004, logging in a grand total of 5,020 hours over the nine years from 1996 to 2004. That, folks, is dedication. It also needs to be pointed out that those hours represent the kind of unsavory work that volunteers tend to shy away from. Namely long days inside an office researching files and deeds, writing applications for grants and permits, filing water right modifications, and.... you get the idea. Not that he was not an on-the-ground person, Bob just made sure all the paperwork was complete before he "pulled the trigger" on the fun stuff outdoors (like building dikes, developing wetlands and securing water sources).

The Grassland Habitat Unit (GHU) was a mix of irrigated grassy meadows, gently rolling uplands and mudflat areas with Saltgrass, alkali flats and saltmarsh. It would take specific management prescriptions for each area. Not a simple task. Add to that a mix of water rights that needed to be assessed, then developed and integrated into a grand plan that gave wildlife the most benefit.

So, where to start? That was where Bob's experience helped to get things kicked off. The water rights were plotted from their source (mostly springs) to their legally described "place of use" on Refuge property. Making matters more complicated, flows from each spring had to be shared through a rotation schedule with private landowners who also had water rights. Some water rotations were not written down, they were just "historic" agreements from who knows how many years back. Then the "government" showed up. I wanted to make sure we were getting our fair, legal share – nothing more and nothing less.

I was worried about how to resolve long standing "gentlemen's agreements" over water use when our water right included more water than we were getting. Bob's research often revealed that the Refuge needed to claim water being diverted by someone else in the system. There is an old saying, "whiskey is for drinking and water is for fighting." In some cases, aggressive landowners just started taking more than their share sometime in the past. For whatever reason they were not confronted by other water users. It is easy to lose use of water when you are not vigilant with protecting your full right, or don't know exactly what it is.

From his exhaustive research, Bob listed EVERY water user on each water right. He could tell me how much water each user was entitled to and where they could take it. Then, the ground work began. Each and every point of diversion, each ditch and each spring (or source) was verified on the ground. From that work, we knew if each "system" was being correctly divided up and used. Guess what. Most systems were not being operated within the legal framework recorded by the Utah Division of Water Rights. Keep in mind, the vast majority of landowners (farmers/ranchers) had never looked at their legal papers regarding water rights. Their rights were passed down through the generations and they just accepted their water supply as it was. Now we came along and actually went back to the legal documents on how things were divided up many decades ago. There were some serious discrepancies and in some cases numerous landowners besides the Refuge were not getting their fair share. I was thinking, "How do you proceed on that as quickly as possible without making a bigger than necessary trauma and still get things straightened out?" I could just see this getting to be a HUGE issue, you know- like that stupid case BLM had over the grazing issue with the Bundy clan. A simple grazing permit violation got elevated into national news and it looked like BLM was unfair to a small time rancher (who happens to be cuckoo).

Bob already knew the solution. First the don'ts: Don't elevate this to the Regional Office or the Solicitors Office, Don't get law enforcement involved, Don't involve the press and Don't try to bully the landowners. Now the do's: Move quickly, Be sure you have correct information on EVERYONES rights, Be fair, Talk to everyone involved (and nobody else), Be accessible and lend a hand if possible to improve things for everyone.

With Bob's guidance, we resolved one "system" of water rights at a time. It started with talking to each landowner in person--just introducing ourselves and explaining we would like to meet with everyone involved together. We played it low key and kicked a lot of dirt clods while we got acquainted. At the evening meeting we had a packet of water rights information for each player that included the entire watershed. Bob, our "expert," explained the legal terms and how the system was legally set up to run. Then we just opened the meeting for everyone to ask questions and discuss their questions. Finally, we would press for an agreement on how the water source would be divided, including a schedule for who gets water for how long on each cycle. I was amazed at how smoothly it went! We held a number of these meetings and they all went well. People actually left on friendly terms. I give Bob the credit for that because he ran the meetings and people knew he was a volunteer, not an actual employee. Bob also gave absolutely correct information and explained every detail in question. We also made it clear that every landowner could double check our information and we even encouraged folks to consult a lawyer if they would feel more comfortable. Funny thing, I could see Bob being accepted by the landowners as an expert. There were a lot of follow-up meetings requested with Bob because he was trusted enough for advice on other questions. Once they trusted Bob, they saw his information as free legal advice. So there you go--one major issue solved at the field station level because of one volunteer! You can imagine how thankful I was.

Bob went on to organize a separate "water rights file" that stood by itself and included photographs of each diversion point, ditch, culvert and other water management facilities under each water right. That, in itself, was a huge amount of paperwork as well as on-the-ground inspections. Joe Saenz was in the middle of receiving his advanced degree in water rights, and so was I!

So, in 1996 and 1997 the official use of water rights began with Bob accompanying Joe on each rotation of water for the Refuge on the dozens of schedules. This was a valuable lesson on what you were supposed to do in taking water from someone else's land and diverting onto your own. Bob knew all the details of how the unwritten rules of getting your water worked. The Refuge fit right in and our neighbors treated us fairly and with respect. We did the same.

Some systems needed major maintenance because ditches were clogged, culverts didn't flow correctly, diversion structures were in disrepair and delivery canals leaked. We met with the other affected landowners and made a plan to do repairs so the system would work better. That was good for everyone – less waste and more efficiency. Sometimes we cleaned ditches that helped get water to the Refuge, but also helped all landowners with receiving their share. That bought us goodwill. Other systems needed new control boxes and Bob designed new structures that helped us and at the same time helped the neighbors. Another act of goodwill. You might say that we were buying friends. Maybe so, but it worked and I would do it again.

By 1998, the preliminary background plans were completed along with gaining the necessary permits to develop six new wetlands. This included building dikes, delivery canals, installing culverts, building access trails and replanting vegetation. A major diversion at the spring identified as Stauffer/Packer was built to help split the water to each landowner according to their rights. We were excited to see the immediate response by wildlife.

Development ramped up in 1999 under a grant from NAWCA (North American Wetland Conservation Act) which we received in cooperation with Ducks Unlimited. The project called for restoring 253 acres of wetlands by constructing six water control structures, rehabilitating three brood ponds, constructing a delivery canal system, installing a diversion box and putting in a parshall flume to measure waterflows. To improve the grassland vegetation winter grazing was prescribed on 722 acres, in cooperation with Utah State University. New fencing was installed to enable control of prescribed grazing. In all, the project took 36 days.

The work continued in 2000 when more diversion boxes were built, buried pipes were installed, 6,700 feet of canals were cleaned and excavated, dikes were built, "waterman gates" were installed to divert water, a 36" water control structure was placed and access trails were constructed. It was a busy spring and summer considering this was all done in addition to what was happening out on the "original Refuge."

In 2001, the GHU was managed without doing more major developments. The water rotation schedules were maintained and vegetation management via winter grazing was continued. Wildlife use was observed and plans were made for another major development effort by applying for another NAWCA grant in cooperation with partners. Applying for and receiving one of those grants is not as easy as it sounds. Partners have to be brought into the mix, donations have to be received and permits have to be obtained. All this, well before construction details are planned (supplies, staff, machinery, volunteers).

It is a lot easier to just sit back and complain about not having money, rather than going to the work of making out an application.

Good new arrived for the 2002 season, we were awarded a $119,000 grant! Those funds were put right to work and things happened quickly on the ground. A new wetland complex was developed consisting of five new wetlands. Work accomplished included building 7,030 feet of new dikes, burying 310 feet of ABS pipe to carry water and constructing nine water control structures. Bob Green was spearheading this project with Aaron Johnson, a new employee. Once again, Bob found himself in the role of a mentor/trainer. It was such a unique opportunity for Aaron and he soaked it in. Bob returned each spring for two more years and assisted with projects on the GHU as well as the original Refuge lands. After volunteering over a seven year period, his fare well was difficult for me personally. As he left, I was moved with gratitude and respect for all his service.

As for the GHU, it became a productive and valuable unit of the Refuge. Providing a diversity of grassland and freshwater marsh habitats, it is used by both resident and migratory birds. It stands as an example of cooperation with other agencies, non-governmental organizations and local landowners.

CHAPTER 26

THE FRIENDS OF BEAR RIVER REFUGE- -A CORPS OF PRIVATE CONSERVATIONISTS

The style of U.S. Fish and Wildlife Service management evolved greatly during the 1980's and 1990's. If you were to encounter a refuge manager in the "good old days," he would for sure be a "he" and his management activities would have been entirely behind the refuge boundary fences. In other words, there was very little effort to involve the general public in management programs. It was a classic case of government people doing government things on government land. They didn't need help from anyone outside-thank you very much! That was it, "cut and dried." Refuge managers could handle their responsibilities without having to ask or rely on outside help. The general public was basically a pain.

Obviously not all managers were that way, but it was the majority thought process. It was an element of our agency culture.

That style worked ok for decades, then it became evident that a private citizen support group or an officially organized *friends* organization could help with garnering support when needed for funding or for public support during controversy. Those refuges supported by Friends groups were more successful in accomplishing wildlife goals than those "going it alone." It became clear that having an organized non-profit group of supporters gave the refuge manager "cover" in times of controversy. Such groups could also support a variety of improvements for wildlife and public use. Friends groups were nothing new to the arena of public lands. Consider the National Park Service, they had the foresight to establish the Friends of Acadia National Park, the Friends of Yellowstone Park and many others. I think our independent attitude in the Fish and Wildlife Service slowed us from believing that friends groups would be helpful to every refuge.

I had no experience with friends groups in my previous refuges, but I knew they could be a big help from time to time. I was all in favor of them, but really did not know where to begin. The story of how the "Friends of Bear River" started is truly another God thing. It sort of just started happening before my eyes and I was being pulled along rather than leading.

The genesis of the friends group at Bear River Migratory Bird Refuge really began in 1989 when Bob Ebeling recruited his corps of volunteers and loosely termed them "The Friends." Right from the start, Bob would say he represented the "Friends" when he was fund raising or asking for goods and services. I loved it and just went along without providing any real leadership. That was all well and good, but there was no official paperwork organizing the group into a non-profit organization. In fact, when people donated money they wrote their checks to the Box Elder Wildlife Federation and the donations were given to Bob. Could that be illegal money laundering? I don't know but it worked. Point is, there was no official "Friends of Bear River." We just pretended! It sounds unbelievable, but it worked from 1989 until 1997. Bob's friends were sort of a ghost group of people who had no leaders, no meetings and no rules. It is even hard for me to believe as I write this down. I guess it worked because we never got questioned. Bob Ebeling was the leader (sort of) and he could look you in the eye and not flinch. So it just worked, that is all I can say. Another example of someone taking the bull by the horns and serving as a ramrod to get something done. It is a good thing we didn't ask anyone in the Fish and Wildlife Service for permission to do what we were doing!

Even with my slop along personality, it was evident we needed to get official at some point. So, in about 1996 I decided it was time to do the official paperwork and incorporate officially for legal and tax purposes (we were not a 501 (C) 3 non-profit organization). Good gracious, that was about seven years of unofficial status and shooting from the hip.

I talked to Lou Heinz, refuge manager of Ding Darling Refuge in Florida, who had a Friends group that raised $1Million for their Visitor Center. I was in awe as he told me everything the group had done for him. Lou gave me some advice about how to officially organize and then put me in touch with Molly Krival, a dear lady who gave her retirement years to help organize new friends groups for refuges all across the nation. So, there you have it. Imagine me with stars in my head about getting Bear River officially on board with the growing number of new friends groups organizing nationally.

REALITY CHECK, this is a painful memory. I failed miserably on the first try. How could I go wrong on a job as easy as organizing something that was already running? By getting the wrong people involved, that's how. I knocked my head around trying to think of names for the first board of directors. For some dumb reason, I thought that getting at least one board member who had only tentative support for the Refuge would be good. You know that old idea of keeping your adversaries close. So I asked four people to help organize the group and become the first board of directors. We had a couple of meetings and talked strategy, then it became clear one member was going to second guess our full support of the Refuge. Doug wanted to call the group "Visitor Center Advocates," rather than the "Friends of Bear River Refuge." He was not comfortable with being fully associated with the Refuge. What a disappointment considering we had excellent community support. I decided to disband the group and lick my wounds for a while.

Then I gave it a second try and I was smarter this time. I took council from two of my local mentors, Bob Valentine and Jerry Mason. For my second start up attempt, they recommended Jon Bunderson for president. Jon was a well known and a respected hunter/conservationist in Brigham City. He served as Box Elder County Attorney and was well acquainted with the government officials in both Box Elder county and Brigham City. His family reached back several generations in the area and he knew a lot of people. He was also known to be supportive of the Refuge. In addition, he had the perfect temperament for leading an organization. He would listen, but knew when to nudge things along so meetings would not become bogged down. When it was time to make a decision, he would lead the group for a vote and get on with it. He had great judgment and a sense about how to interact with the local people and local government. A great choice all around, but would he accept the position? Jerry and I went together to his law office and popped the question. It was as easy as that, Jon accepted my request and it turned out to be another defining moment in the success of the "not-yet-established" organization. Jon knew the ins and outs of the legal paperwork and to get it submitted to the IRS. The other big bonus with Jon is that we really worked well together and I enjoyed him immensely on the personal level. I guess you would say that made us "regular friends and Friends of the Refuge." Was this the good Lord at work again, looking out for the Refuge and me?

We needed some sort of public event to get the official Friends of Bear River Refuge organization started. In the spring of 1997 we decided to have a festival and officially launch the organization. We made a big deal out of it. There were activities all day long around Unit 2. Wasatch Audubon helped staff observation stations at several pull offs. Browning employee Dave Reynolds brought his trained dogs and gave demonstrations. We held a raffle and also had a silent auction with donated merchandise. Activities went on into the evening with a Dutch oven supper followed by presentations from Terry Tempest Williams the well-known author of the book "Refuge" and Congressman Jim Hansen. I remember it as a day full of energy and when we closed things up late that evening, I was really played out. It was a good kind of exhaustion because we had accomplished our goal of getting the public out to the Refuge and featuring the "Friends of Bear River Refuge" as an official organization. Now we were on our way!

Maintaining our successful start to the Friends group was also due to the addition of Jay Hudson to the board of directors. Jay was a retired administrator with organizational skills. In addition to being an avid naturalist, he was politically connected in Ogden and had a long history of being involved in community affairs and civic organizations. Right away, he volunteered to ask the Swanson Foundation for some start-up funding. We soon received $5,000 from Jay's request, that gave us some resources to set up our organization. Jay also recommended the Friends publish a monthly newsletter to get our activities out in the public eye and help build the organization. We settled on the title "Migrations" for the newsletter and Jay was the initial editor.

Now the Friends of Bear River Refuge could start an official list of members and receive dues and donations. Our very first charter member was – I need a roll of the drums--- volunteer Bob Green. He donated $1,000 to show his support. At about the same time, Bob Valentine made a similar donation. Our first "official" meetings involved setting long term goals. We talked about towers and other improvements, but the thing most on everyone's mind was a Visitor Center.

The concept of replacing the flood destroyed visitor center dated back as far as the Environmental Assessment of 1992, but it never went anywhere. It was something that everyone seemed to be in favor of, but the Agency had no funding and so the concept just floundered. That is, till the Friends of Bear River Refuge board of directors started talking up the concept and decided they wanted to ignite the effort to get a Visitor Center built. The board wanted to shoot high. Their concept was to go for a first class building and have a topnotch education program with it. They were not happy with planning to do something cheap and quick. It was going to be first class all the way. And me, well I had no idea of what was ahead (clueless again), so I said "You bet. Lets' go for the best." Being ignorant of what you are biting off really can be bliss. I had no clue on how difficult it would be to buck the system. Heck, for that matter I had no idea of what we were going to have to do at each step along the way. It is comical today when looking back on how simple I thought this was going to be. You just put out a can, get some money and then hire a contractor to do the building and, presto, there it is. Right. Boy was I about to get an education AND have some of the greatest experiences of my career. Together, we would be challenging the highest levels of the U.S. Fish and Wildlife Service who did not have any plans to build a visitor center at the Refuge. Getting on the agency's list was a highly political process and we simply did not have their attention, or frankly, any of their concern. The Friends of Bear River Refuge were soon going to show up and smash the status quo.

The Friends of Bear River Refuge became an extremely effective organization and I give the credit to Jon Bunderson's leadership. He had excellent judgment and was goal oriented. He also had a steady hand and knew how to keep the organization focused on the most important issues. For example, Jon felt the organization should refrain from getting involved in controversial issues because that would dilute their focus and effectiveness. He was looking for maximum support from a broad base of individuals and organizations, that meant staying out of negative campaigning over some political issues. Jon would go on to hold the presidents' position throughout the restoration. That lent an important quality of stability and recognition. Jon was the face of the organization. Above that, he was a trusted personal friend I could count on for solid advice and personal support.

Likewise, Bob Valentine did an excellent job with his main responsibility on fundraising, communicating with agencies and developing effective political connections. Lee Shirley was our connection with Audubon and the various public user groups. John Kadlec was our connection with academia and some of its key players. According to guidelines from the national friends group coordinators, elections for president and directors were recommended annually. We ignored that, and for good reason, we had a cohesive team doing outstanding things-why mess up? I also served on the board, something else not recommended.

The Friends of Bear River started a newsletter "Migrations." Jay Hudson was the initial editor and ramrod. He did a great job and sent the publication out to all the members on a regular basis. Jay also filled the position of director for a period of time. After the organization showed success, we were contacted by the National Friends organization and asked to help with mentoring other fledgling groups around the country. Jay and I were asked to attend some initial training and join a team to visit other areas. We spent several years with the mentoring team and got to meet numerous other groups trying to get started. All the visits took me many miles away, and I proudly told people that traveling more than 200 miles from home automatically made me an expert. Actually, I think if I helped at all it was to encourage others that they could do it.

With Lee Shirley's encouragement and guidance, we began an annual "Bear River Bird Festival" that became a popular event. When Davis County decided to do a similar event, "The Great Salt Lake Bird Festival," it unintentionally competed with our festival. We decided to let them take the lead and involve tours of Bear River Refuge into their festival. That avoided conflict and created some good will. Since we were a featured destination, it worked out just fine. Lee's heart was always for public visitation, be it birdwatching, sightseeing or hunting. He just wanted the public to have an experience on the Refuge. Years after the restoration, 2018, an observation tower was built and dedicated to his memory.

In 2002, Bob Valentine accepted the position of chairman of fund raising. His "magic" involved leading efforts toward the gigantic goal of raising funds for the Education Center, a $1.5 Million goal. That story is legendary and involved partnering with Box Elder County, Brigham City, private foundations, non- governmental organizations and the general public. I will save that story for the next chapter.

The Friends of Bear River Refuge and I developed a close and trusted friendship. At monthly board meetings I would take time to explain all the current management activities and anything else that was on my mind. Some might say that I was too transparent with "inside" information, but history shows that it worked well with this board. I never regretted sharing information. On the contrary, the board helped with all my matters of concern time and time again. I also had frequent conversations with the individual board members when I wanted their opinions on something they were experienced in. When I had issues with political roots, my phone rang into Bob Valentine's very frequently. Looking back, I relied so heavily on Bob, Jon and the other board members that it may have made some of my

AL TROUT

higher level staff feel left behind. After staff meetings when we were discussing a problem, I would frequently say "I'm going to give Bob or Jon a call on that before I decide." If I had it to do over again, I would do it the same way! My advice to other younger refuge managers is to go out and develop some trusted local "Friends" and use them. It is so much better than going-it-alone.

In subsequent chapters I will tell the more detailed story of how the Friends of Bear River Refuge made the Education Center possible. Other high profile accomplishments were paving the Refuge access road (in excess of $20 million) and persuading the Department of Transportation to build the Interstate on/off ramp at Forest Street which gave Interstate 15 traffic direct access to the Education Center. Other accomplishments included funding teacher positions for environmental education and obtaining "earmarked" construction funds.

The Friends of Bear River Refuge accomplished a wide array of projects over and above what we could do with the federal Refuge budget. It was just plain fun to do projects underwritten by the "friends." There were no formal applications to fill out and submit for approval and no extensive budget reports to fill out along the way. It was as simple as talking over a proposal at a Friend's board meeting and getting their approval. They had the authority to write a check for the Friends' on the spot. It was that clean cut.

Examples of the variety of accomplishments include constructing a viewing platform ($15,000) on the Auto Tour Route; purchasing furnishings for the Education Center; and supporting bird festivals and children's art contests for main street banners. The Education Center construction budget was falling short, so the Friends purchased the flagpole through a donation from employee John Peters. The list goes on—educational programs, symposiums, wildlife research and walking trails. But perhaps most vital were annual grants to hire staff to assist Kathy Stopher with environmental education programs reaching thousands of students.

When I decided to set a retirement date (May of 2006), I made the announcement at the last official board meeting before my departure. Without skipping a beat, Bob Valentine spoke out "You're not going anywhere fella." He made a two-part motion. Part one-he nominated me to become an official board member immediately upon my retirement. Part two-I would be in charge of making a film for the education center auditorium. The motion passed unanimously. Anyone else hear the train whistle? I was also given the go-ahead to spend up to $100,000 to get the job done. How is that for an assignment?

That meant I entered retirement as the junior member of the Friends of Bear River Refuge board and an assignment that would take me two years to complete. That is another story which will be covered in chapter 30 "Wings of Thunder." It turned out to be another experience in doing something I knew absolutely nothing about and leaning on the board in the process. Looking back, I would not have it any other way.

CHAPTER 27

POINTE PERRY-YOU CAN'T WIN 'EM ALL

During the restoration, not everything turned out exactly the way we wanted. Pointe Perry is a prime example. If you look west as you drive along Interstate 15 and see this ugly conglomerate of a cheap motel, gas station and general store, just remember it looks EVEN UGLIER to me. Here is how it came to be. This is a long, painful story. Please keep in mind that I am not opposed to private enterprise, commerce and people making money. I am opposed to the destruction of wetlands and wildlife when it is totally unnecessary and especially when it does not even make sense from a business point of view. Ok, with that off my chest, here is a brief sketch of how and why Pointe Perry exists.

When we established the proposed new Refuge boundary at the beginning of the restoration (see chapter 16), the east boundary of Refuge lands was planned to butt up against Interstate 15. Why the Interstate you ask? That wide strip of black top would make a clear-cut boundary between the wildlands of the Refuge on the west side and the urban development of Brigham City and Perry on the east. Right off the bat, we were successful in acquiring several parcels of land along that corridor from willing sellers and felt good about prospects of acquiring more as landowners became willing to sell at their own pace. These grasslands mixed with small wetlands are rich in wildlife. By the same token, these low elevation lands are marginal for buildings because of wet, unstable soil conditions. No locals were proposing development and the Brigham City long term plans called for leaving this land alone for eventual inclusion into the Refuge (once again, on a willing seller basis). Development of this area would be expensive and isolated from other businesses in Brigham City. It was simply not a good business venture considering the location and engineering costs. I should say, it would not make sense to any private investor using private dollars to invest them for the potential returns. How do you spell "bankrupt"?

The plot thickens as "Craig" comes along. He ran a company called Enviroserve. This out-of-town environmental consultant was retained by Box Elder County to inspect wetland areas and propose a plan to both protect some high quality wetlands and yet allow some industrial/urban development as needed. He was telling the County he could come up with some win/win ideas that the Environmental Protection Agency would agree with and allow the County to offer would-be commercial interests some development options. A crafty solution like that would be good news to the Box Elder County Commission. Unfortunately, his inspections and analysis did not render any plans or solutions in the areas he was supposed to be inspecting. His observations did, however, render for himself a completely unrelated idea that would be extremely profitable for himself. Good bye Box Elder County wetland plan, hello out-of-town developers.

Craig noticed that the west side of Interstate 15 was wide open agricultural land, including the off ramp at 1100 South. Where he came from (Salt Lake City area), all intersections like that were prime development sites. So, he hatched a bright idea to contact some of his out-of-town developer buddies and get them interested in purchasing a parcel of land on the West side of the Interstate for commercial pads. Never mind that the Refuge had already purchased several parcels in that area, including half the land around the interchange. This development was getting muddled up right from the get-go.

Craig was all smiles (a well groomed guy with great speaking ability) and told the Perry City town council how good a development would be for their tax receipts. The Perry City fathers were ill equipped to digest the presentations by experienced developers like Craig. He told them what they wanted to hear. The first step was to have the area rezoned from agriculture to industrial uses. Pretty quick, a majority of the council members were in favor of the development. It really went downhill from there over the period of a couple years. Craig's first developer friend (Crowley) came up with the idea of getting Cabela's to build a new store in the area. BIG SPLASH. Wew, Cabela's!! Craig introduced himself to me and wanted the Refuge to jump on board to promote the great idea. Excuse me, I like Cabela's as much as the next outdoorsy guy; but I just would not, could not, get behind any development in that area. Unfortunately for Craig, Crowley and their investors, I was talking down their pet idea. That angered Crowley and I received a letter from his attorney demanding I apologize and mend my ways or I would be sued. My comments were costing the would-be-developers money. As a side note, the letter made it sound like the Cabela brothers were bosom buddies. Except one thing, he spelled their name "Cabellos!" You would have thought they would at least have looked at a Cabala's catalog. I consulted the "Friends of Bear River Refuge" President Jon Bunderson (remember he is an attorney) and he said, "just ignore it". And I did.

This issue went on for what seemed like forever. Their purchased lands were full of wetlands and could not be developed without a permit from the U.S. Environmental Protection Agency. Since they only owned about half of the land surrounding the exchange, they really needed the other half which the Refuge owned. The nearest utilities were in Perry and it was going to be an expensive, time delayed process to get the area ready for development. Much of the area would also need to be drained and then filled with several feet of soil. Behind my back, they made a run with the Congressional Delegation to have the land they wanted removed from the Refuge and made available to them. It didn't work, thanks to our good friend Jim Hansen, but it really torqued me off. If I was in their way before, now I was an outspoken critic. My hackles were up and I intended to be a pain every way I could.

More time passed, more publicity and lots of bologna. Then one fine day, Lanning Porter introduced himself and said he represented the NEW owners of the proposed development. Lanning was a recently retired Air Force officer and was hired by Rollie Walker (from Idaho) to spearhead the process. Lanning was a nice enough guy, but completely green regarding the Refuge and associated wetland issues.

Lanning tried hard to put his best foot forward, but he had a lot of background information to absorb. Since Lanning was a nice guy, just uninformed on federal wetland regulations, I allowed him to take a lot of my time explaining the hurdles he faced. If I had it to do over, I would not have given him so much time. I soon met Rollie, we walked the area and I was straightforward in telling him not to follow through with the purchase of the land because it would be a real headache to him – and me too. Rollie ignored my advice and soon was officially pushing ahead with development plans. Sure enough, it was one problem after another.

I would like to string out one excruciating detail after another, but it would probably bore you to tears. Overall, Rollie and his legal team somehow sweet talked Perry City into footing the bill to have utilities brought into the site. That was huge! Rollie had the taxpayers of Perry partially on the hook as well as his own investors. Brilliant on his part and sorry to say, not so brilliant on Perry's part. Rollie was able to purchase additional lands from the Staffer estate by contacting an out-of-state heir. Rollie had enlarged the footprint of the development to 90 acres, greatly increasing the potential impact to the Refuge and its' wildlife. I started losing sleep for the first time. Of all things to really get upset about, this non-resident developer was getting the best of me. He could spread BS like nobody else. Lots of people had his number, but he was slick and persistent so he usually maneuvered around opposition.

It was time to take stock in how to best neutralize this problem. The choice came down to an all-out opposition of the development, hoping we could still prevail and make Rollie walk away from his investment. In order to put that much pressure on him, I would have to convince the Army Corps of Engineers to deny Rollie a permit to build over wetlands. The Army Corps of Engineers had jurisdiction in regulating wetlands. I worked with them all the time. They had the power to stop the development, but it was questionable if they would or not. They could allow development through a complicated "miti-gation" process. Once again, I called my good friend Bob Valentine and we decided to make a personal visit to the office supervisor of the Corps of Engineers. He could not assure me that the Corps would stand in opposition to the development. There was a possibility, but not anything close to assurance. That left me without much of a "club," or a "big stick," as Theodore Roosevelt would say.

I huddled up with my most senior staff, Vicki Hirschboeck and Steve Hicks. They were both "up to speed" on the issue. We needed to decide whether or not to oppose the development, or to strike the best deal we could for the Refuge. If we opposed and lost, the entire parcel of land would likely be developed. That would be painful to the entire Grassland Habitat Unit. If we defeated Rollie, the development would just go "belly up."

On the other hand, if we proposed a sort of cease fire on the condition that the development be limited in size and that the Refuge be allowed to purchase and trade out for his remaining land, we could ensure that the pain would be limited. So, to go for broke or to make a deal to ensure limited impact, that was the question. It was a tough decision. I was glad to have a great staff to lean on. We wrangled back and forth among the three of us, but we finally made the unanimous decision to cut a deal.

I called Bob Valentine and told him the direction we wanted to go. As always, Bob was on board with our direction and vowed to help us however he could. I leaned on him plenty through the negotiations. Bob's incredible knowledge of all the players, including both federal and state agencies and politicians were invaluable. There were more details than you care to read through, believe me. Through it all we limited the extent of the ugly damage and managed to add some valuable habitat to the Refuge Grassland Habitat Unit.

When it was all said and done, we did ok for ourselves when you consider how bad it could have been for the Refuge. I was just used to winning big on most things we got involved with. I think it was due to finding common ground with all the players. Usually, we could find a way for everyone involved to come out with something they would gain. But, Pointe Perry was another matter. The Refuge lost its undeveloped eastern boundary. And, guess what? Pointe Perry went into bankruptcy a few years later. That means the investors Rollie pulled in (i.e. suckered) lost as well. It would have been better for everyone if Craig had never shown up along with his developers and subsequently their investors.

Lesson: you can't win 'em all; pick yourself up and keep moving forward.

I still want to say, "Told you so" and neener, neener.......

CHAPTER 28

THE EDUCATION CENTER, "YOU ARE NOT IN THE PLAN" and "YOU CAN'T DO THAT"

In 1983 the Refuge proudly dedicated a new Visitor Center at the headquarters site near the mouth of the Bear River. It was a lovely site, being surrounded by thousands of acres of marshes and untold thousands of migratory birds. At the grand opening ceremony, dignitaries from far and wide were there to show their support for such a fine facility. It was an immediate hit with the public as well. Visitor use was robust and it was a success right from the start. When fall arrived, it started to snow and snow and snow. Then it snowed some more until every record was broken. When spring of 1984 arrived, the record snowmelt fed all the rivers running into Great Salt Lake. Lake levels rose slowly, but inch by inch month after month the lake rose until it surrounded this new facility. Even though coffer dikes were built to protect the building, the persistent waters managed to slowly infiltrate and destroy the new building. No one would have predicted that untimely demise in just months after it was dedicated.

While making plans for Refuge restoration in 1990, a common theme among the public was to replace the destroyed Visitor Center. The public loved it and for good reason. A well designed visitor center enhances the quality of a trip to the Refuge. Visitors can talk to a real person, there are exhibits to see and current information is available. It was inevitable that we have a new visitor center on the drawing board as part of the restoration. So, as part of our official approved restoration plan signed in 1992, there it was in black and white. We just had to change the name to "Education Center." Why? For political purposes the regional office informed me that Congress did not like visitor centers anymore.

They were only funding education centers. OK, whatever. Sometimes you just go along with things when it doesn't really matter. After that, I trained myself to say, "Education Center." The general public, however, still referred to it as a "Visitor Center."

Right off the bat it was clear that no funding was available to even think of starting construction. The special purse of "Construction Funds" for these kind of projects is very hard to come by in the Fish and Wildlife Service. As several years slipped by, we were never even included in the five year construction list. Simply put, Bear River was never going to get money for the Education Center in my career. But, being the eternal optimist, I went forward with some preliminary planning to select a site. We selected a site just a couple miles west of Brigham City on Forest Street, close to Interstate 15 and still above the floodplain. It was easily accessible to the public, unlike the original Visitor Center located another 14 miles west. The new site would attract more visitors since it could be seen from the highway. We also developed a sketch of an example building and estimated the required size to meet our needs. The total cost estimate rang in at a whopping $14 million. That number shocked me, but I figured it was something we could throw out and then decrease as reality dictated.

Remember, my outfit did not handle big numbers well. I joked that the motto of the U.S. Fish and Wildlife Service was, "if you think at all, think small." This was not a small project by any stretch. I was also a bit overwhelmed by the size of the proposal because it was something I had never done before.

When you propose building an Education Center, you also need to develop an initial interpretative theme. Oh man, I hated the thought of doing that. It was just one more hurdle that required stopping to develop more plans. It would require endless hashing over just exactly what we wanted to convey to the public, what we wanted to be the theme of our exhibit hall and how we would carry out the education programs. With the help of a specialized consultant, Consortium West, we decided to focus on the concept of the refuge being a "meeting place." We would develop the concept that the Refuge was the hub where the Bear River from the north met Great Salt Lake from the south and wildlife from the west met civilization on the east. Like most of the planning we did, I liked it after we finished! It smacked of common sense because it not only involved the no-brainer elements of wildlife, wildlands and the River, but also the reality of managing people and civilization as part of the equation. Like it or not, people were here to stay.

So, there we had it: a proposed site, a basic interpretive theme and a cost estimate. Even though it was just a rudimentary start, it was something. I need to remind you; all this planning and background work took lots of time and effort. Since this was our big idea, the Regional Office did not give us additional staff to do the work. My exceptional staff and volunteers sucked it up and just added it to their already overfilled plates. It was truly a shared vision among the entire staff and the "Friends of the Refuge" organization.

When it was all done, I placed that paperwork on the shelf and hoped to revisit it someday. But at that time, it was no use to push on it without a funding source—or at least a shot at a funding source. Besides, my staff was stretched thin doing the rest of the habitat restoration that was going full tilt. I had no staff to assign to this as their primary project.

The challenge ahead of us was on several fronts. Funding always comes to mind first, and that was overwhelming to me as a Refuge Manager inexperienced in the ways of the Washington appropriations process. Let's just say it was convoluted, confusing and a lot like making sausage (something you don't want to watch before you eat it). It has a life of its own and only the experienced bureaucrats can navigate their way through it and come out with money. Everyday people like me just get run to death when engaging the system. That is why so many good ideas never become funded.

When you are fortunate enough to get funding, you enter an entirely new world ruled by government regulatory offices of various types who control every segment of the project. For instance, the Office of Engineering takes control of everything dealing with construction and design. Then there is Contracting and Generals Services (CGS) They control all the purchases and contracts to private construction companies. Then you have the Office of Safety looking over your shoulder with a rule book that must be a foot thick, while Human Resources double checks and places restrictions on who you can and can't hire. The Office of Personnel takes control of every hire and they have a process that grinds along at a snail's pace. All your funds also must go through Budget and Administration and so on. It just makes getting anything done more complicated than it has to be. That is one reason so many agency employees just do their assigned jobs and go home. It makes life much easier. However, my staff was not wired that way. Neither were the "Friends of the Refuge."

Another challenge we were faced with was the ever-present time sump that this project would be. As it progressed, the Education Center would require increasingly more time and effort.

I hope you are ready for another God thing, 'cause here it comes. In 1995, after the background plans had been languishing on the shelf for several years, I got word that a new refuge supervisor had been assigned to Bear River. The Regional Office called a big meeting in Keystone, Colorado for a few days so they could explain a new reorganization and pass out new supervisors to all the Refuge Managers. OK, this happens every so often with the Federal Government, so off to Keystone I went. When I found out that my immediate supervisor and his immediate supervisor were NOT long time Refuge people, I flipped and said some unkind and stupid stuff. By the way, I later apologized for what I had said (I was the stupid one). Larry Shanks introduced himself as the new boss to a bunch of us refuge managers (he was from Ecological Services) and his boss, Joe Webster, who was from Fisheries (a "fish squeezer" to me). Told you I was ignorant. Through the test of time, these two guys turned out to be superb, and just what was needed to benefit refuges. They saw our old problems in a new light. Go figure.

We would later nickname Larry "the bulldog," and that was meant as a compliment because he did not blink or back down when he was doing something FOR us (not to us). Larry was direct and goal oriented. He had a warm side and liked to operate on friendly terms, but he was mainly out to get something done. He would not entertain whining for the sake of whining unless you had an idea of how to solve your gripe. At the Keystone meeting, Larry gave each Refuge Manager a few minutes to talk to him alone and brief him on issues or say whatever you wanted. I knew most of the other managers would use the time to cry and belly ache about no money, no staff, bla bla bla...

I made a brilliant decision (for once) and decided to give Larry a copy of our restoration plans and tell him all about what we planned to get done rather than gripe about how bad things are. I had no idea how he would respond to my presentation because I was throwing out a challenge rather than just an information briefing and gripe session. I got my chance for the presentation after he had been worked over by a couple of guys I knew to be classic complainers. With plans in hand, I spent my time telling about the good things we were doing and long-term goals we wanted to accomplish. I ended the presentation by saying we were going to build an Education Center as part of the restoration. Well, there is a whopper for you. Ending a presentation with saying we were going to build a $14 million Education Center. Silence, silence and a little more silence. Then Larry asked a few questions for clarification and the meeting was over. At least he didn't laugh me out of the room, I reasoned to myself. On the other hand, I did not expect him to do much about my own Refuge problems, like a lack of money and staff to build an Education Center.

Unbeknownst to me, Larry would soon be the one leading efforts to achieve the funding goal. But before that happened, I answered a call from Bob Valentine and "out of the blue," he suggested we talk to Congressman Jim Hansen about the Education Center. Well, OK. That was a subject I was afraid to bring up because Hansen had been so good about getting us money for dirt work each year and I did not want to make a huge request that would blow his mind and make him think I was getting greedy. Bob, however, preferred to be right up front and see what Jim thought about the project. Bob got us an appointment to meet Jim at his "cabin" in Farmington one evening. When we sat down, I had the concept plan with a sketch and the estimated costs. Bob led the way. After a few minutes of small talk, Bob turned our attention to the Education Center proposal. Jim listened and asked for the price tag. I was scared but acted calmly and said,

"14 million dollars." I waited for a reaction as he mulled it over in his head. Then he asked, "Can you guys come up with a million and a half?" He continued, "If you can, I will come up with the rest." I didn't know what to say. Raising $1.5 million was more than I could wrap my head around, so I glanced over at Bob sitting to my left. Bob didn't hesitate and said we could do it. That was good enough for me and I chimed in by agreeing. We shook hands, thanked Jim for his support and walked out to my car in the evening air. I looked at Bob and needed reassurance that we could do it. Bob was already thinking about people he could get involved. His energy got me cranked up and we chatted all the way home about fund raising in the private sector.

For the next little while nothing happened because I had no idea how to lead the way. Although we had Jim's support to go after federal funding, I had a new hurdle: raising $1.5 in private funds. I had lots of experience in spending funds, but none in raising that kind of non-government money. I floundered in my ignorance. How was I going to move ahead on two fronts of fundraising: federal and private? The answer was about to come in unexpected ways.

I was headed home from the Refuge one day and was flagged down by Alan Esplin, the manager of the Canadian Goose Club. He told me one of his members, Steve Denkers, was in the clubhouse and wanted to talk to me. You never know what it will lead to when someone wants your ear and you are a Refuge Manager- it could be good or bad. I pulled into the parking lot and went inside the clubhouse to find Steve. He walked up to me, cigar in hand, and asked bluntly, "When are you going to start the Visitor Center?" My quick reply was, "When I can raise one and a half million." Steve gave an instant retort, "That's a cakewalk." I was stunned and didn't know how to react, so I just stood there looking kind of dumb. That conversation would turn out to be the start of our process to meet our fundraising goal. The full story is in Chapter 29. For now, just know that the private fundraising efforts were going on concurrently with the efforts described below to gain the federal funds we needed. The overall deal was that we needed to get $1.5 Million in private funds and at the same time get $12.5 million in Federal funds. Interesting. I had never done anything of this magnitude on either side of the equation. Are you sick of hearing about this being a God thing? Well, just keep reading

My telephone rang one fine morning and it was my boss Larry Shanks on the other end of the line. He said, "pack your suit and call Bob Valentine because we are going to Washington." Then he said, "I'll show you how to run the tunnels" and "We are going to get that Education Center funded." Ahhh ok, I replied. Larry had met Bob Valentine on a previous visit to the Refuge and knew immediately he was a huge asset for us. He also recognized Bob's political strength across a broad spectrum of federal, state and non-governmental organizations.

My assignment before the trip was to prepare a briefing statement that I could present in seven minutes. I was to be ready to answer all questions that involved Refuge operations, including use of funds and accomplishments and whatever else may come up. One strict rule, I had to play the party line and under no circumstances was I to ask for any additional money. I was remined by Larry that I worked for the President (he is head of the Executive Branch) and when he signs the Federal Budget he is telling the world that the budgeted amount is sufficient for the Refuge. I was not free to say we need more or to request anything. End of story. If I were caught doing that, Larry said it would be grounds for dismissal. Goodbye career!

Larry's role was to navigate our path through the U.S. Fish and Wildlife Service, The Interior Department, The Office of Management and Budget, the Senate and the House of Representatives. Not a simple walk through the park: this venture was going to take some administrative and political know-how. Guys like me get eaten and thrown out on day one. It just gets overwhelming if you don't know how to get through the maze.

Bob Valentine's critical role was to speak on behalf of the "Friends of the Refuge" and the citizens back in Brigham City and Box Elder County. Bob's unique background included being a County Commissioner; Director of Economic Development; Director of the Utah Division of Wildlife Resources; President of Utah Wetlands Association; Director of Utah Reclamation, Mitigation, Conservation Commission; Director of Ducks Unlimited and, trust me, a slew of other stuff. Bob knew everyone who had a political, economic or conservation impact in Northern Utah. He helped on campaigns to elect Senators Hatch and Bennett as well as Congressman Hansen. He also made reasonable cash donations to their campaigns. Bob was the only person I knew who could call a senator's office and actually talk to the senator or congressman. Try doing that yourself sometime. I predict you will talk to a staffer because the real guy is always "out of the office" for people like us.

Larry gave me a list of people we needed to meet with. Wow, it was a laundry list of agency people, senators, congressman, nongovernmental agencies (like Audubon), and others I would never have guessed like OMB (office of management and budget). I set up meetings with the Fish and Wildlife Budget Office and The Interior Committee on Appropriations, the National Wildlife Refuge Association and a bunch of others. You get the idea. I set up meetings, one after another, with just enough time in between for the three of us to get where we needed to go (walking and cab rides).

The first day of our first trip started at Arlington where Rick Coleman, the director of National Wildlife Refuges had his office. Picture Bob, Larry and me all in suit and tie. We arrived on time and Rick, with a friendly smile, invited us in his corner office. He was fairly young, energetic and passionate for refuges. His enthusiasm was such that he advanced the refuge cause beyond what his supervisor was comfortable with. Later on, when he was told to throttle back his efforts to advance the refuge system, he resigned rather than do a less fervent job.

After Rick's greeting, the three of us began the presentation and a special "chemistry" developed. I enjoyed every minute watching Bob connect at the community and political level. Larry had long-time connections with the agency personnel. They gave me the confidence I needed to be at ease, yet still on my game with current Refuge issues. Larry led the way with our intentions. He told Rick we were there to put funding together for the Education Center. Valentine lent support from Brigham City, Box Elder County and Jim Hansen. It was just good plain fun as the meeting cranked up with enthusiasm. Rick ended our meeting by giving us his blessing to go after the funds, with only one caveat, any funds we gained had to be "new money." That meant we could not pull money from other refuges to enrich ourselves. Any funds we received had to be newly appropriated from elsewhere --hopefully a long way from the Fish and Wildlife Service. I had no idea how to make sure that did not happen, but Larry was the expert on those matters, so I just fell in behind his guidance.

We left Arlington and immediately picked up a cab and went to the Interior Building, located "on the hill." When you arrive on Capitol Hill, you enter a different world. Even back then there were security checks at every entrance. It was crowded, full of energy -- people just seemed to be on task doing something. I had visited D.C. before but never to do business like this. It was just different and seemed confusing and chaotic. We checked into the Interior Building and a security officer asked where we were going. We replied that we were headed to meet with the Fish and Wildlife Service Director and with staff in the Budget Office. An officer called ahead (even though I had my badge) and then told us to go ahead. The Director, Jamie Clark, welcomed us in and we repeated our brief and informative presentation. Bingo. She likewise gave her approval of our plans. With one meeting after another lined up, we proceeded directly to the Budget Office. There Larry was greeted with energetic hellos and hugs from Pam Hayes. She called her immediate staff together as Larry explained what we were going to do. I was already lost by this point, not knowing the players or what they did. Half the battle is knowing who to listen to and who to ignore. I had no idea. This was Larry's realm and he was steering us through the maze already. I just answered Refuge questions and invited everyone out for a guided tour.

As we ended the meeting, much longer than the first two, we were given advice that Larry told us right afterward to ignore. One of the Budget Office staff declared "Bear River Refuge is not on the books," and then went on to say, "You can't do that." From his perspective he was right. Problem is, he had no idea what Larry had planned for contacts and furthermore, he had no clue as to the depth of influence Bob had. Gary's comment was to become a repeated source of humor over the next few years. Whenever we made progress toward our goal, we would declare, "you can't do that!" It brought a lot of laughs over the years.

Larry was the guide as we threaded our way through various House, Senate, and Department of Interior offices. Our list also included a variety of non-governmental offices like the Audubon Society, Nature Conservancy and The Cooperative Alliance for Refuge Enhancement. We even went to the Office of Management and Budget to make sure they would lend support. Larry guided our efforts through this complicated budget system and made sense out of what seemed to me as chaos. As for me, I was lost in a whirlwind most of the time. I just tagged behind Larry and Bob and tried to fake like I knew what I was doing.

The government offices we visited were a world unto their own. Schedules were tight and there was constant tension to keep strictly on schedule because every minute counted. It was obvious that these people had carved out a precious few minutes to hear us. I saw it as a brief and unique opportunity to make an impression. It was a case of having one shot to get our point across. A quick, well presented request showed respect for their time and attention. Our presentation was honed to the minute. I started out with a six-minute presentation using a booklet with graphics and pictures. Occasionally Larry would kick me under the table, a signal for me to wrap it up ASAP because he could see we needed to move faster. In any event, we kept on eye on clock as well and excused ourselves in 30 minutes as a matter of respect.

We were also prepared to give presentations in the hallway and on "the fly." These presentations were necessary when our appointment was cut short by unforeseen circumstances – an all too frequent occurrence in D.C. We had to get our point across while walking down the hall and handing off our briefing booklet. To my surprise, it worked when it had to. When it all boiled down, the people who worked in this pressure cooker atmosphere really did want to be a part of something in the real world that made sense. And that is just what we tried to offer them.

The briefing booklets we used were state of the art for that time. Vicki Hirschboeck and Karen Lindsay deserve credit for investing a lot of time and energy into making these attractive and professional. I spun my presentation off these booklets and left copies in every office. They told a story in photos and graphics. When I completed my segment of our presentation, Bob Valentine took over with his discussion and provided additional paperwork of his own. I fell silent during this part because it involved the request for funding that I could, under no circumstances, lend personal support. That would get me reprimanded in a New York minute. But, this is where Bob absolutely excelled. He could negotiate and sift budget numbers without hesitation. His requests could be broken down to a list of line items that he was prepared to justify. His demeanor was calm and professional. Because Bob was doing all this as an unpaid volunteer, his words and actions held even more weight. How could you find fault in someone who was investing a huge amount of time and effort into a project benefiting the general public? In his "real job," Bob spent a career in the aerospace industry as a negotiator and it was fun for me just to sit back and watch him in action. No razzle -dazzle; he was simply a master at the art. The best part of it was that Bob always, and I mean always; told the truth and if he made a promise he was sure to follow up on it. He was well respected by those we met with and we frequently ran across people that had met Bob through the years when he was a Commissioner or Director.

Larry rounded out our trio by playing a key role in representing the Regional Office and giving credibility to our effort from the Agency standpoint. Earlier in his career, Larry was stationed in Washington D.C. and learned how to work the system. Since he was my direct supervisor, his presence lent an air of approval by the Fish and Wildlife Service. Larry also maintained an open channel of communication with Ralph Morgenweck, our Regional Director in Denver. Larry could address any questions about how the Education Center would fit in with Regional goals. He knew the key agency players from bottom to top and how all the government offices worked together (or not).

After a few runs, we became a well-practiced team. On top of that, we were genuine personal friends. That made all the difference in maintaining our high energy through this process, which was going to be a long haul over several years. It was just plain fun and exciting.

On the frustrating side of this process was how our own Agency tripped over itself. The Regional Office in Denver had several divisions that became involved just because that was how money and responsibilities were divided. In other words, the division of Finance was involved with all appropriations that came into the Agency, no matter how they arrived. Then, the Division of Engineering was involved with building design, whether we wanted them or not. When it came time to actually build something, GSA (General Services and Administration) took charge in writing contracts, soliciting bids and selecting contractors. That would have been all well and good, BUT each of those offices represented a bureaucracy of their own with processes, rules and numerous personalities.

Getting what we wanted from them on time was a whole other matter. It amounted to losing control of the project while it was in the "giant's gut."

Normal protocol was for an architect to be selected by the Division of Engineering working in concert with the Division of Contracting. That sounded fine, but in reality, we had an initial meeting with the architect to explain what we wanted. We got to describe the size, function and some general details, then the architect went off on his own to develop a building design that he thought made a statement. I had hoped to sit down with the architect and help develop some sketches. No way. We didn't hear from the architect for weeks; then we got a proposed design that costed us money if we wanted to modify it to any major degree. The architect wanted to claim the building as his design, not ours. I know the process would have gone more in my favor if I had been more experienced at this.

Remember, this was my first time at riding herd over a building project of this size. It proved to be a challenge!

Likewise, the Division of Contracting and General Services had their realm of control. They took over the process of writing and awarding a construction contract. That sounded reasonable, but we got a process that moved ahead at the speed of a snail. They had other projects to do and we just had to wait our turn. I did not cope all that well with delays. By the time our project went out for bid, my fingernails were bitten off for several months (time is money in construction). Then they wanted to do wacky things like set aside your project for minority contractors only. Noooo. That means you limit the competition to companies that cannot compete in the open market and win a bid. It drove me nuts because we were trying to stretch our funding as far as possible, not be a government welfare program to help minority owned construction companies. I was all in favor of encouraging minority businesses to submit a competitive bid. I just did not want to pay more than necessary for a contractor. Does that make me a mean person? Don't answer that.

More of the same thing went on with the Division of Engineering. They were supposed to inspect the plans once the architect submitted them. In my experience, they took a lot of time and still did not catch all the mistakes in the plan. Once Engineering accepted the plan, any mistakes became the responsibility of the government to fix. You guessed it, that meant more money from "my" budget. The list for normal operating procedure went on. I wanted to select the person to be construction inspector, but that turned into a power contest with Engineering and CGS. I lost, so instead of having someone we knew was good, that position was advertised nationally and they selected the applicant they wanted. Engineering also provided construction estimates and they could put a hold on the project whenever they thought funding was inadequate. In our case, they delayed the start of construction one year because they thought our available funding was inadequate (wrong, wrong, wrong). By delaying the start of construction, however, total cost of the building materials actually rose $1 million. By blundering around with some relatively small budget issues, they insured the loss of big bucks! I went nuts again. That made me mean and crazy. We had worked like crazy to come up with the funding and every dollar meant something to us.

I could go on, but you get the point. Because of all the "safeguards" put in place by the intricate processes of the bureaucracy, the cost of construction went up automatically. Projects progress slowly and most of the time you do not get to select the best companies for the job. To complicate matters, our Education Center was NOT funded through the "normal" process, so it was even more problematic to a system designed for doing things "by the book."

Our goal that first year of going to Washington was to just show up in the budget anywhere for any amount. Larry knew that if we had some level of appropriation, then we could return to Washington the next year and ask for another increment toward the goal. That was experience and patience talking. After doing all we could and investing the best effort we knew how to make, all we could do was go home and wait until the budget was made public. At that point, we had made all our contacts and could only hope that in our absence there would be a consensus to throw some funding our way. We waited. And waited some more. I was on the confident side that we would get something; I just had no idea how much to expect.

Then came the day when the budget numbers were released to the Regional Office. Larry was the first to look over the list of funded projects and then he called me. Here it was, the moment of truth. Larry simply said we did NOT make it anywhere in the budget at any amount. In other words we completely struck out. That's right, shot down in flames. Man was I discouraged. That was a lot of work for nothing, and even worse, I had convinced myself that we were making a great impression in our meetings. Now I had to conclude that my best efforts were just not that great. Well, BooooHoooo on me.

Larry pulled me back into reality and was not about to let me sink into gloom and doom. "Be patient," Larry said. "We made a lot of good contacts and we are not giving up. "In Washington you start an appropriation process by kicking a rock off the top of a hill. You just keep kicking it until it starts to wiggle and move. Once it starts to roll then it will go all the way to the bottom by momentum." Larry's pep talk gave me the hope I needed to give it another try the next year. As for Bob Valentine, he was all-in.

We repeated our efforts the next year. Timing is critical to be effective in the budget process. Too early and they forget about you; too late and the budget die has been cast. Larry knew just the right week to go and he told me to set up all the meetings again. Starting up with the Fish and Wildlife Service Director, we were told that we could give it another try but we had some major hurdles in front of us.

OK, so we went down the hall to our next meeting in the office of the Budget Director. We got no encouragement there. It was a bummer for me, but Larry was unphased. We just sucked it up and kept going down our list of appointments.

We made repeat visits to all the offices and players we had contacted the first year. Although we did not get much encouragement, the people remembered us. I think we made an impression because we did not give up after striking out the first year. Persistence does make an impression. This year, Bob Valentine also brought news about the private donations that were flowing into the "Friends of the Refuge" for this project (remember, our goal was to raise $1.5 million). The Willard Eccles Foundation gave the initial contribution of $250,000. Other contributions brought it up even further. That war chest showed we were making a big effort back home and had local support. It gave us a degree of credibility and it did make us feel a little more bullish. It was a two-edged advantage. Receiving government appropriations gave us leverage in raising private donations; and, conversely, it helped when we reported to government officials that we had private money coming in.

We made it a point to schedule a meeting with Congressman Jim Hansen each time we were in Washington. He always gave great encouragement to our effort and made us all feel like personal friends. Jim took extra time with us just to visit and find out how things were at the Refuge. He usually had a story or two about his early years duck hunting with his father on the Refuge. I always felt relaxed around Jim, he was a genuine guy and he did not seem like the "typical" politician—whatever that is. I considered him a key player in the process. We were supercharged by the time we left his office.

We faced another major hurdle when we met with Loretta, Chairman of the Natural Resources Committee. She held a key position in determining the projects that would be funded in the Interior Department. She was a tough cookie, but I also think she was fair and had a difficult job. Every day someone was asking her for more money, so we must have looked like everyone else. Loretta remembered us and listened politely. She said we needed to downsize the plan substantially and then maybe we would have a chance. I had no way of disagreeing with her request/order to downsize. Larry was also in a tough spot and couldn't do too much. Not so with Bob Valentine. As a private citizen and volunteer, he was in the perfect spot to let his opinion known. His superior command of negotiating led the way. He could disagree without offending and lend perspective until consensus was reached. He let Loretta know that the "Friends" would look over the project and "scrub the numbers." By taking this tact, we were able to move ahead with our requests to all the other players. Over the ensuing months, Valentine was able to firmly hold the line for us. I just kept my head down and let Bob take the lead.

We did go back home and review the plans and numbers again to see what could be modified or eliminated. Since the size and design was driven by the building's proposed function, we were not going to give anything up (that is, Valentine was going to hold the line for us).

About that time, Larry found an additional funding source in the Department of Transportation. WOW. The DOT goes through billions, and getting into their coffers would be a big help. Larry was always keeping his eyes open for opportunities like this and a "small program" called T21 was available to help with public access if a list of criteria could be met. Of course, we were masters at meeting whatever criteria needed to be met. For example, there had to be an existing parking lot and access road. We really did not have a parking lot, but it only took me one day to make one-all by myself. All it took was laying a few old utility poles on the ground and mowing the grass where cars, in theory, could park.

Viola, there is your parking lot. We were able to get $750,000 that we could use on the Education Center entrance area. We then happily decreased our overall budget request by that amount and it helped make Loretta more supportive.

We had additional meetings with Loretta since all projects had to go through her. At one point, we seemed to be at a stalemate and she was not placing our project on her list of approved construction items. We talked to Jim Hansen and he sent his senior staff member, Alan Fremyer with us to meet with her. There must have been a history between Loretta and Alan because he seemed irritated at Loretta right from the start. After some discussion about costs and other priorities in the Department, Alan said, "Either you put Bear River on the construction list or Jim Hansen will introduce a bill to authorize the funding," Loretta was a bit taken back and replied, "Well it looks like we have an additional project on the list." It was that quick. One minute we were in limbo, the next minute we were on the official list. We did not know how much we would get, but at least we were written in. I was overjoyed. It was also very humbling to see the support Bear River had from Jim Hansen and Bob Valentine. They were making this happen. I was just a very happy spectator.

We left our meeting, which was attended by several dozen people, and met a familiar face in the hallway. It was Gary, from the Fish and Wildlife Budget Office. When we made our first visit over a year before, he had commented to us, "You can't do this, you were not on the list". There he stood, just hearing the news that we did do it and we were on the list. Gary looked at me and said, "I hope you are happy, you got your way." I took that as a compliment, but I'm not sure how it was meant.

After all our visits the second time around we came back home and waited for the new budget to be released. It was a different story this time. I received the good news while I was involved with a presentation to the Division of Fisheries in Denver. I was helping with an explanation on how to develop a friends group; similar to the Friends of Bear River Refuge At the break I received a call from Larry telling me that our project had received $1.5 million. Yippee! That was enough for us to get started right away. Our first step was to finish some engineering and architect work so we could put the project out for construction bid when the rest of the funding came in.

We were up to our ears in plans, design and raising private funds when it came time to go back to Washington a third year. We prepared in much the same as before, but our reception in Washington was totally different. By this time everyone knew "Bear River" and we had a place in the official budget documents. Yes, the rock was rolling down the hill just as Larry had predicted. Our job now was to give a good, accurate account of the funding we utilized. We also were prepared to show how Engineering estimates were aligning with the initial cost estimates we used for the Education Center. That was not as easy as it sounds. With each passing year, construction costs went up. Also, architects would design features in the building that could affect the cost. When redesigns are needed to reduce construction costs: the associated time delay can eat up all the savings through inflation. These kind of things got frustrating. We even went through a "value engineering" review where I spent time in Denver going over the plans with a team of engineers looking for more economical construction methods. Nothing came of this intense exercise except another delay in the overall project – and more lost to inflation.

When it was all said and done, our initial estimates for the cost of the building held tight and we requested the same funding levels as in the first two years. That is good news. Washington budget people absolutely HATE it when you start changing numbers. Larry knew that and we did our best to keep all numbers the same. What did change were our conversations with all the players in Washington. By year three they were familiar with us and asked, "How are you doing this year?", "What happened since last year?", or "what is your status?". It was a given that we were going to get more funding. It was only a question of how much. As it turned out, year three was a big year; we received a significant increment of what we needed. We had more work to do, but progress was steady.

In all, we visited Washington 5 years and had more fun every year. We had progress to report each time on the Education Center as well as the private funds we were receiving. We were nearing our goal of $1.5 million and that was a success story in itself. The Washington people were pleasantly surprised that we were making good on our promised effort to raise the private donations. Really, it was Bob Valentine who had made the promises and was delivering just as he said he would. That whole experience was, in many ways, the pinnacle of my career. I also know it was a highlight of Bob Valentine's "retirement" and Larry's career. It was as good as it gets. We had managed to meet scads of people who held positions in various agencies and elected officials as well – including Senators Bennett and Hatch.

A few years later in an audiotape, Larry said, "you have a few things in your thirty or forty-year career where you are in the right place at the right time and there is just some wonderful, fantastic people chemistry. Each person has different strengths adding to complement each other. We were fortunate in that particular time because we had a good political environment and the chemistry was there along with the interest. And, the Good Lord made it happen and we were blessed with a facility."

A year before we received our last increment of funding, Larry retired. What a loss when he left our "team!" When he said farewell at his retirement dinner, he told me, "Don't let murphy get you while I'm gone." Larry went on to explain that years ago he was put in charge of constructing a facility for the World's Fair in New Orleans with very little time. He got the job done, but had to "break every rule in the book" to do it. Larry ended the story with some advice for me, "When you go down that road, you can count on Murphy's law to come up and bite you, so don't get discouraged." I was well aware that we were bending (ok, maybe breaking) a lot of rules but things seemed to be going along just fine.

What could possibly go wrong??

We needed one more appropriation after Larry retired, so Bob Valentine and I repeated the Washington visits for another year to complete the project. That was a more difficult year. In addition to loosing Larry and the chemistry he brought to our team, some employees within the Fish and Wildlife Service started to push back. They didn't push back before because they would have to go eye -to-eye with Larry and he had the "machizmo" to quiet them down immediately. Since I was from the "field," it was impossible for me to go to battle with them on equal ground. Plus, I don't have Larry's "bulldog" personality. I wound up catching a lot of flack from people who thought we had too much money and that our facility was too large. Never mind that we had raised $1.5 million of private donations.

The overall budget climate had changed in Washington by then. When we started the process four years earlier, there was a surplus in the federal budget. As the budget fell back in the red, though, people were looking closely for funds they could tap (or "steal"). We had accumulated around $8 million in advance of construction starting and that got a lot of attention. We needed just one more increment of funding and we would be set to go. There was more blood – letting over our last request than all the others. I remind you, our last request was no surprise because we had not increased our budget one cent over the years. We held the line on inflation because we knew how bad it looked to start increasing budget requests. Since Larry was gone, it was an invitation for anyone within the Agency to grouse or do what they could to hinder our progress. All of the petty issues that Larry use to handle now fell on me. Larry's replacement, Steve, was inexperienced and only mildly supportive. Our issues were over his head since he was a newly appointed refuge supervisor with only field experience and no Washington savvy. I was on my own – except for the support of Bob Valentine (and that was a huge benefit).

Once, Steve called me and said the Regional budget had no allowance for the annual utilities that the new building would require and this was going to be a big problem. I replied that we were currently paying over $100,000 yearly in rent for our second rate office facility. I told Steve to take that pile of money and move it over to pay the utilities. I thought that was a great solution. But no, Steve said that wouldn't work because that money had already been obligated elsewhere. Losing patience, I told Steve we could either work together to solve this or I could just tell Congressman Hansen that we would not be opening the new building. Of course this problem eventually got solved, but someone in the agency wanted to make a point by making me sweat. It was just irritating and Larry would have squelched these kind of petty issues before they ever reached my desk. It was as if some regional staff in the division of finance were saying "You worked around us, now you need our cooperation and you are not going to get it."

However, we did have champions in the Regional Office that were always supportive. Regional Director Ralph Morgenweck and Sherri Fetherman, Chief of Visitor Services never wavered in their support. Even though we went through some rougher times during the final year of appropriations, I think most of the Regional personnel gave us a fair shake.

Our final hurdle before construction came from within our own agency at the Regional Office level. Our final appropriation had been added by Washington and we were ready to proceed with advertising for construction bids. Our "estimated cost of construction" was a number generated by the Division of Engineering. They used a list of nationally averaged costs of each building item to come up with a total for what they say the building should cost. The grand total cost from these estimates was slightly more than what we had in our total appropriation. I was not concerned because construction costs in the Brigham City area were below the national average; we had seen that time and time again with smaller projects. In addition, we were in a construction slump and several large construction companies were prepared to put in competitive bids because work was scarce.

Instead of going ahead with bidding, one zealous administrator in the Regional Office decided we needed to "replan" and come up with enough savings to lower the Engineering estimate to exactly equal our appropriation. GEEEZZZ. OOHH NOOO! So the progress toward starting construction was brought to a halt while a replanning process was started. You would think that a quick replan could be done in a few weeks. It would be like trimming here and there and maybe eliminating something that would bring the cost in line. That was not what happened. The process took a full year because it involved rewriting contracts with architects then getting on their schedule. Then the proposed changes went back and forth between Engineering and the architect and the Refuge. When it was all said and done, we lost $1 million due to inflation of construction costs. We had to cut even more. It was very frustrating. It caused us to cut out an entire maintenance building to meet budget, just because we did not move ahead earlier. I was really frustrated at the way our own people shot us in the foot.

Even so, we finally moved ahead with advertising the construction bid. It was awarded to HHI Incorporated and we had a groundbreaking on June 23, 2003. Construction began with a huge amount of concrete work that took months to form and place. Supervising the construction was a huge, all-consuming job for several of us on staff. It required our continual attention and it seemed like we dealt with a "crisis" every day. It was another God thing that Steve Hicks was my deputy manager. Steve was very confident in himself and skilled at construction. The contractor was always looking for any part of the plans or contract that were ambiguous or had an omission. That was his chance to submit a "Change Order." A change order was the contractor's key to the federal treasury because they were allowed to remedy the so-called problem through a non-competitive bid. They just totaled up a cost for the work and it was ok'd, even for ridiculous amounts of money. Steve, on the other hand, doggedly supervised every step of construction. He held contractors to every facet of the requirements and when necessary he stood his ground. He held the number of change orders to a minimum because he usually found a way to negotiate through an issue. Steve might allow an alternative construction method or material that was an advantage to the contractor in turn for an equal consideration when the government plans or specifications were lacking. Truth is, the contractor really didn't much like Steve. I thought he was the perfect person for the job. The Regional Office had actually hired a professional inspector who was on duty full time, but Steve was a better negotiator for the government interest.

In regard to how the building was named, it was an idea that Bob Valentine and I hatched one day. We decided that Congressman Hansen needed to be recognized for the unwavering support he gave the Refuge. This was another case where I didn't ask the Regional or Washington Office what official protocol was for naming things after people. I just announced that the name of the building would be the "James V. Hansen Wildlife Education Center" and started using that name. Nobody told me I couldn't do it. Congressman Hansen was appreciative and it was a good move. It needs to be recorded that Jim did not in any way hint he was helping us with the Refuge so his name would go on the building. It was totally our idea to honor him.

I also wanted to honor Bob in some way, so later on I named the auditorium after him and his wife Joan. Likewise, the exhibit hall was dedicated to Steve and Susan Denkers who provided the initial private funding.

Finally, it was time to start building! We pressed on with construction for 18 long months. Because this whole thing was our idea, the Fish and Wildlife Service did not provide additional staff during construction. We just had to suck up the extra work in addition to our regular duties. The staff did it willingly because we were all excited about what was happening. We could hardly believe in January of 2006 that the building was complete. It was a strange feeling to receive the keys after the final inspection one January afternoon. Steve and I stood alone after the contractor left the building for the final time. It was quiet and the winter sun was setting. We just quietly walked through the building as darkness settled around the snow covered landscape. We had done it. A chapter was closed and a new chapter was about to begin as the Refuge was entering into a period with new possibilities in education and management. My head was stirring with thoughts about how different things would be in the future. My heart was full of gratitude to the many people who had made this possible and the journey we had experienced together. I was especially aware of God's hand in bringing all this together.

CHAPTER 29

IT'S A CAKEWALK

The Education Center started as a dream. Scarcely had the ruins of the Refuge emerged from the receding floodwaters when a cadre of volunteers and supportive citizens cast the vision for a restored and improved Refuge. Those people envisioned a bigger, more productive Refuge for wildlife plus a world-class Visitor Center to better serve the public. That vision, unofficial at first, developed on paper over the following years to become an official proposal.

Some initial sketches and designs served mainly to help cast the vision to the general public during the early years of the restoration efforts. A concept plan for the Visitor Center-soon to be termed an Education Center for political reasons-was developed next. Copies of that plan were available to the public, but not much happened beyond that for an extended period of time. The plan was just laying around on the shelf and, worse yet, we were not even on a long-term construction plan anywhere in the Agency. In reality, it was going nowhere.

Then Bob Valentine brought about a sudden change of events. He suggested we initiate some action on the Education Center by meeting with Jim Hansen to request his help to get some funding. WOW. That was exciting news for me because I knew Bob had the influence to make big things happen. "Yes," I said, "I would love to meet with you and Congressman Hansen if that would be possible." Bob explained that he would arrange a meeting next time Hansen was in Farmington at his "cabin." Indeed, Bob lined up a meeting and we explained to Jim that we had a $14 million concept plan with no present funding. Jim thought for a few seconds and then made a deal with us right there. Looking across the table at us, Jim threw out the terms of a deal "If you get $1.5 million and I will get the rest."

Terrific! What a deal. Except for one thing. I had no idea how to raise that kind of money. Sure, I had raised some small-time funds for various organizations, but nothing close to this. As we drove back home, Bob assured me that there were ways we could get the job done. Deep down I believed Bob and I was glad he had confidence, but I was totally unsure of myself. So, for the next little while, I made no progress on the funding. I was not sure how to initiate something, so I did nothing. I think God was lining up the next big break. He usually waited to bless me until I realized it was something I didn't know how to do on my own.

Steve Denkers, part owner of the Canadian Goose Club (a neighboring hunt club) and Director of the Willard Eccles Foundation, told Alan Esplin (manager of the club), that he wanted to talk to me on opening day of the duck season. I was always doing law enforcement on the Refuge on opening day weekends, so I was not hard to find. Alan found me and said Steve was at the clubhouse and wanted to talk to me. That was puzzling. What would Steve possibly want to talk about? That afternoon, I zoomed over to the clubhouse about 5 miles down the road and pulled up outside the clubhouse in my Refuge truck. I had a good relationship with most of the members as well as the manager and his helper-volunteers. I normally showed some bravado by yelling, "federal raid!" and getting everyone's attention. I was greeted by a member or two who said Steve was inside, so I stepped right in. Kicking back after a half-day hunt, Steve was at the bar smoking a cigar and tipping a mixed drink. He was also in shorts-the opening day weather can be in the 90's. Steve and I were on good terms, but I had really not done much serious business with him. I had given the club some advice on water rights applications and I know they appreciated that, but not really much else.

Steve is a direct sort of guy. He said "hi," we shook hands and he got right into what he wanted to talk about. "When are you going to build that Visitor Center?" he asked. I was a bit taken back because I didn't know he cared or even knew anything about it. I took a second and fumbled around for something to say and replied, "When we raise one and a half million dollars, Hansen promised to get the other twelve and a half million and we will build it." I expected a critical reply over that amount of money, but he didn't hesitate in replying "THAT'S A CAKEWALK!" I was dumbfounded and probably looked a little funny just standing there trying to process his statement. I had no idea how to raise that much money and Steve called it a cakewalk. Here I go again, about to get eyeball deep into something I knew absolutely nothing about raising big money in the world of foundations. I bumbled around for some more conversation tid-bits before excusing myself. I made no plans with Steve, nor did I get clarification of how he thought we should proceed. I was just blown away with someone of his caliber thinking it was a doable project. So I did what I always did when I was hit with a big challenge I knew nothing about, I called Bob Valentine to tell him all about it.

Bob listened and calmly said "Call Denkers and set up a meeting." I did just that and we were soon in Steve's office talking about how to go ahead with fundraising. He said he would go to the other members of the Willard Eccles Foundation and convince them to give a healthy contribution to get the project going. Steve explained that we needed a big kick-off donation to help get other foundations to follow suit. We planned a Refuge airboat tour for the other members of his board on the day of their annual meeting. We let them use our conference room after the airboat ride. Several days later Steve called with the good news. We were approved for a $250,000 gift! Wow. That gave us some credibility for approaching other foundations. It was a great start, but we still had a long way to go.

We were excited to get such a marvelous donation right from the start, but that immediately begged the question of what to do next. Bob and I went back to Steve for more advice and a direction of where to focus our efforts. Steve said we should go to the George Eccles Foundation next and talk to "Lisa." He smiled and picked up the phone (an antique desk model hooked to the wall with a cord). He got right into Lisa and told her he was sending two friends over to talk about Bear River Refuge. She gave us an appointment and that was that. About a week later we were in the First National Bank building looking up her office number and we just couldn't find it. We gave Steve a quick call for directions to her office just minutes before our appointment. After we described the surroundings on the floor we were on, Steve said "that makes no sense, where are you?" "Right here in Ogden at the First National Bank", we replied. Steve burst out laughing. "Lisa is in the Salt Lake City branch, not here in Ogden" he replied.

Steve retold that funny episode many times over the years and it brought lots of laughs. We quickly called Lisa and rescheduled our meeting. Next time, we were on time and in the right location.

We introduced ourselves to Lisa, then got right into describing the project. Bob did most of the talking because he represented "The Friends of the Refuge" and that was what impressed prospective donors most. Bob was an unpaid advocate who was obviously putting a huge amount of personal time and energy into the project. That spoke volumes. Lisa listened politely and asked, "How much did the Willard Eccles Foundation donate?" We replied "$250,000." She sat quietly for a few seconds and said, "We will give you $100,000." I could hardly believe my ears! No application, no waiting, no red tape, just

15 minutes of conversation and we get all that money. WOW, this was really getting to be fun! As we said our goodbyes, Lisa told us to pick up an application on our way out and send it back so they would have the information needed to donate the funds. We couldn't wait to get back and tell Steve the news.

So, back we went to Steve's office a few days later to give him an update and ask what to do next. The three of us enjoyed basking in the good news and then we asked Steve for suggestions. He picked up the phone and arranged for us to have an appointment with the Mariner Eccles Foundation. That meeting went well, but we did not get funding to use for construction. Instead, we were told to request funds for educational programs after the center was up and running. Fair enough, it was good to have a contact for the future to expand our educational programs.

We picked up momentum along the way as a variety of donors made contributions. Appendix 1 lists the major donors in alphabetical order. Some of the donations came as a big surprise from private supporters like Gary Slot (manager of the Bear River Club) and several of its members like William Morris and Zach Brinkerhoff. Substantial gifts also came in from Friends' board members John Kadlec and Bob Valentine. The money was an exciting gift in itself, but the demonstration of their commitment had an even greater impact on me. It all added to the excitement and momentum of our effort.

We returned to Steve's office for yet more advice. This time he said that Browning should be good for a donation and he knew Don Gobel, the president. Steve made another call, right into Don's office, and moments later we were scheduled for an appointment. Arriving at the Browning Firearms plant for our appointment, Don introduced himself and invited us to join him and a few of his staff around a table. After some discussion, with Bob taking the lead to describe how the "Friends" were raising $1.5 million, Don explained that Browning was not able to donate much cash at that time. He explained that gun manufacturers were being sued by various anti-firearm groups and legal fees were eating away at cash reserves. However, Don said he wanted to help and had an idea.

He pulled out a pamphlet that featured a presentation grade Browning shotgun and told us that a similar group had just raffled this gun for over $50,000 and he was willing to have one made for us. It would feature one of a kind engraving and be serial numbered 1 of 1. WONDERFUL. We just got the promise to have a special shotgun gifted to the "Friends." Once again, no muss or no fuss, just a simple presentation by Bob and we received the commitment from them to manufacture a special shotgun for our project. Bob and I were excited to have Browning involved; it would just give us one more major donor to boost the credibility of our efforts.

We reported our success with Browning at the regularly scheduled monthly directors meeting of the "Friends of Bear River." This is another place where President Jon Bunderson navigated us through some really tricky legal landscape. Jon, a practicing attorney, knew all- to-well about the prohibition of gambling and lotteries in Utah. So, how could we do an *unlottery* lottery? Jon had to "officially excuse himself according to the official minutes" so we could get down to how we could proceed below the Utah legal radar. We came up with a convoluted solution, we would not sell lottery tickets as such. NO, NO AND TRIPLE NO. We would accept "donations" and then put the donor's name in the drawing. Their name would go in numerous times according to the amount of their *donation*. "Illegal," you say? Probably so, but it worked because nobody complained. As for Jon, he was completely unaware of what we were up to and never offered advice on how we could circumvent the letter of the law. That's my story and I'm sticking to it!

Organizing the drawing (remember, not a lottery) was a lot of work. After we received the shotgun, we needed to design a pamphlet that could be mailed or distributed otherwise. Browning offered the services of an advertising agency they were familiar with. They worked with us to design an attractive publication which featured the engraving. The pamphlet also explained the project to raise money for the Education Center.

We started distributing pamphlets and visiting outdoor shows and events put on by conservation organizations. Our progress was slow and we still needed to get more pamphlets distributed. Bob Valentine stepped in once again with a great idea. He proposed to call the Director of the Utah Division of Wildlife Resources and get permission to use the data base of names from hunt permit applications. That would be tens of thousands of names with addresses. As you could guess by now, Bob was granted access to the data base. Surprise, surprise – not really at this point. Our next hurdle was to figure out the logistics of mailing all those pamphlets, how to receive the donations and how to hold the drawing. Lots of detail there for a few of us who had never run a lottery -oops there I go again- I mean a drawing involving a lot of money. Bob came up with the solution. We would ask the private organization that does the big game drawing for Utah to handle this project. The company is "Wildlife Services" headquartered in Fallon, Nevada. So, Bob and I jumped in the car and drove to their office to talk in person. We hammered out the details on mailing out the pamphlets – how many and when. We firmed up the process of receiving the money and finally how the drawing would be accomplished. When we left Fallon we had a date and place for the drawing and a schedule for tens-of-thousands of pamphlets to be mailed out. All that, and we were not going to have to lick and mail a single envelope. It would all be handled by a professional company at a rock-bottom charge.

Once the mailings started, donations started coming in. We really had no idea how much to expect in this volume mail effort. Remember, we were all inexperienced. Our donations were building into multiple thousands, but we wanted to use all our options. It was time to make contact with the Bear River Club. We had a great working relationship with Gary Slot (manager) as well as the directors and numerous members. They improved the financial landscape of the drawing immensely. Member Dick Heckert decided to purchase enough tickets-oops, dang it I forgot again-I meant to say he decided to make a large enough "donation" to give him a good chance at winning the drawing. He donated $50,000. One donation at a cool 50K. That about blew me away.

The day of the drawing arrived. It was held in conjunction with the annual bird festival at the Refuge. The drawing was computerized and we had folks gather around at the appointed time to watch the button pushed which was programed to select a random number from all the entries. Once the button was pushed, it was programed to delay several seconds – just to add some drama. If you know anything about computers, it could have selected the random number in a fraction of a second, but we wanted it to look more like the computer was working hard to be "random."

AND THE WINNER WAS – Dick Heckert. We presented Dick with his brand new, one-of-a-kind Browning over/under shotgun. Now here comes another amazing thing. Dick accepted the gun and contacted Bob Valentine soon thereafter and wanted to donate the shotgun back to the Friends of the Refuge organization. Dick explained that he took it on a single hunt and felt it needed to be on display at the Refuge. In the months following, Browning had a display case made and the shotgun was put on permanent display in the Education Center.

Donations, both large and small, were coming in at a steady pace. There is a story behind each one. I was invited to attend the annual meeting of the Utah Wetlands Foundation. This elite club boasts members from the Bear River Club as well as numerous foundations across the state. I was chatting with members during the social hour before lunch – they were all well-to-do businessmen. I noticed David, he was head of a major foundation. As I shook hands and began visiting, Steve Denkers strolled over and interrupted. "When are you going to contribute to the Bear River Visitor Center?" he asked. "The Willard Eccles foundation donated $250,000." David was taken aback for a second by the forthright challenge. He hesitated momentarily and said this request was a little late because their donations were already done for the year. "But", he said "I will see what I can find." I just stood there dumbfounded because I could never get away with talking that way to those people. To my delight, David contacted me with a $100,000 donation shortly thereafter. Wow, that was fun just to see how that echelon of people interacted. I was gratified that the Refuge had advocates in all corners of society.

By 1999, Bob Valentine reported to the board of directors that we were about halfway to the fundraising goal. John Kadlec (professor at USU and board member) said he had an idea. He knew people at the Quinney Foundation because they donated to Utah State University and he had done some wetland consulting for them as well. John said he would write a personal request to the Quinney Foundation. It was just one short paragraph requesting they consider helping out. John also mentioned that he was donating time and money to the project. CHA-CHING. We received word back that they would give $100,000. Are you kidding me? That was just a short note, not a 50 page application!

I had another idea to run past Bob Valentine. "How about making Box Elder County and Brigham City partners at $50,000 apiece?" I just picked those numbers out of my head, but Bob agreed to take a run at the City and County. Bob knew "everyone" and he connected all the dots. We attended Brigham City Council meetings along with County Commission meetings. Bob made presentations and answered all the questions. I was along for support and to back up what he was saying. When Bob worked the political system, he was at his best. He was comfortable, confident and straight on. People just wanted to jump on board when he invited them to participate. When it was all said and done, both the county and city made commitments for 50K each!

As we began to close in on the goal, we could say a wide variety of donors were doing their part. We had private citizens, foundations, city and county governments involved. We even had a donation from the Fish and Wildlife Foundation – a quasi government/private fund.

During our last trips to Washington D.C., we were able to say we had essentially reached the $1.5 million goal of private funding. That inspired the various governmental offices to support the last increment of appropriations we would need to begin construction. It had been a long path to collect all the money we needed, but a very rewarding experience. When put into perspective, the "Friends of Bear River" raised more funds (both private and governmental) than any other Friends group in the nation. But then again, it was no surprise to me! Does this seem like a God thing to you? It seemed like it to me!

As a side note of interest, I made it a practice to send out *handwritten* thank you cards the same day that any donations were received. I also made it a point **not** to use government stamps. I bought real stamps from the post office. Jon Bunderson also sent thank you cards. I got a call one day from a donor who enthusiastically said he got my thank you before he even knew his foundation had sent the donation. Then he said I must have had a good family to teach me the simple act of expressing thanks. He said that many of his donations were never acknowledged. We received more donations from his foundation through the years. Mom was right; you should say "thank you," especially for cake!

You never know when obeying your mother's advice will pay off!

CHAPTER 30

WINGS OF THUNDER

I don't exactly remember when I first started thinking about retirement. I loved my job and going to "work" was a joy. My staff was getting along well, the Friends were fully engaged with our activities, the Education Center was under construction and we had great support from Brigham City and Box Elder County. In addition, we had wonderful relationships with our Senators (Bennett and Hatch), and our rock-solid Congressman Jim Hansen. What could be better for a refuge manager? Strangely enough, I had heartburn with my own agency. After the retirement of my immediate supervisor, Larry Shanks, the political climate in the Denver Regional Office took a turn for the worse. Support was generally lacking for Bear River and it was a pain to get cooperation. One example comes to mind: I received a call from my new supervisor Steve, who was ok, but he was not the advocate for Bear River that Larry had been. Steve informed me that there was no money for the utility bills that the new Education Center would require when it was completed in the near future. Problem. I could understand that money was tight in our organization; it always was-the U.S. Fish and Wildlife Service was not a high national priority. I thought for a moment and suggested that the money we were paying for rented office space ($100,000 annually) could be redirected to utilities and the problem would be solved. I was kind of proud of myself for such a clean-cut solution. Steve's quick retort was "no" we could not do that. "Why not?" I asked. He gave me a foggy answer that I didn't buy. I got the feeling that someone in the Regional Office wanted me to sweat, so it got a little heated. "Then we have a choice Steve," I replied, "We can either work together to find a solution or we can call Congressman Hansen and tell him we are not going to open the Education Center because we are broke." That phone call ended on a sour note. Needless to say, that issue eventually worked itself out, but I wondered why the problem had to be thrown at me that way. There were other similar issues on a regular basis that just made me weary. While most refuges suffered from lack of political and local support, we were golden. Why was my greatest challenge with my own people? It did irk me. If only Larry Shanks were back, he would do some serious "eye to eye" in the Regional Office and get everyone onboard – "or else." I was powerless in that arena. I was eligible for retirement at age 55 and I started to mull it over in my mind. The more I thought about it, the better it sounded.

As time went on, I convinced myself that I was a short-timer. I felt that I was not qualified for the job I had created over the years. It became a job that required more administration and less hands-on activities. I loved being out and about with the staff. Paperwork was always something that I minimized. That balance was rapidly tipping in favor of paperwork, paperwork and more paperwork. My mind was made up in favor of retirement when I received orders to institute two new database programs that were supposed to improve maintenance operations and property inventory records. Both of these databases were touted as tools for our agency to request more funding for congress. Wrong. I could see the failure from the get-go. Since I had 35 years of experience behind me, I could predict that it was only going to drain each refuge of staff time and give nothing in return. In regard to the maintenance data base, it was going to require one maintenance worker (25% of my force) to report what the other three employees were doing. That sounds ridiculous, but it is true. I just could not bring myself to do that. It was a total waste.

The final straw was when a support group for the National Wildlife Refuge System lobbied in Washington D.C. to increase the funding for all refuges. Their efforts were rewarded with a $1 million dollar add-on to the national budget. That may not sound like a lot for other large agencies, but to us it was a helping hand. When our Washington leaders decided to take the money and update our computer network, it really frosted me. I couldn't believe that our leaders were so out-of-touch that they would bundle up the entire add-on and throw it into the black hole of computer technology. We had nothing to show for all their efforts – no new lands purchased, no habitat developed. Nothing!

That was it for me. Maybe I was looking for excuses, but that was my turning point. I announced my plans for retirement. Once that decision was made, I got really sassie and enjoyed my tenure as short timer.

We finished construction of the Education Center in January 2006. We had a ribbon cutting in February and in March we had a Grand Opening. Those were great events and they bring to mind wonderful memories. I retired in May on a high note. On my last day of work, I started the day as usual by mixing with each of the staff for a few minutes. It was my time to make sure they were ready for the day and had no hang-ups that needed my attention. I got to Aaron Johnson, a young energetic manager that always had something going. When I found out he was going to do some fox control around Unit 2 for the sake of nesting ducks, I told him to come and get me when he was ready to take off. So, I spent my last day at work out in the field with Aaron doing something to enhance bird production. We drove back late in the afternoon when the other staff were gone from headquarters. It was nostalgic to wish Aaron the best and walk away on my final day. I never regretted it. I never looked back.

When I attended the last Friends of Bear River Refuge board meeting as refuge manager, I asked for a few minutes to update the board on current issues. Jon Bunderson was president and ran the agenda of the meetings. I really enjoyed being at all of the board meetings that I could. They were a great group of people and we fed off each other for ideas and projects. They were my lifeline to the community and much more. I owed them more than I could ever repay in terms of support and advancing my career.

I ended my presentation that evening by letting them know I had plans to retire and wished them the best as they continued on. "That was that," I thought as I took my seat. "Wait just a minute" came the voice of Bob Valentine. "You're not going anywhere fella." I was puzzled for a second, then Bob made a motion to the board "I move that Al be appointed as a member of the Board of Director of the Friends immediately effective upon his retirement and that he be put in charge of producing the Refuge film." There was a quick vote by the directors and I found myself voted in as a future board member.

For several months we had been discussing the production of an introductory film to show in the new Education Center. We were batting around some ideas, but none of us had ever produced a film before. We were doing our best to gain some traction, but progress was slow to this point. I was finding myself once again in charge of something I knew absolutely nothing about. Man, that sounded like the past 35 years of my career! I needed the good Lord to show up on this challenge-- just like He had so many times before.

I figured we needed to line up a photographer first thing, since this was going to be about filming wildlife. Brilliant. A pivotal moment was about to happen and we had no clue of it. My retirement date came and went and I had more time on my hands (good thing).

We put casual word out to a few close associates who were in the photography world, letting them know we needed a good (or great) photographer for the film. I figured it would take well over a year to get all the images we would need. We needed someone with a good track record who would be willing to work hard at making this something we could be proud of.

I was really enjoying the newfound freedom of working as a member of a non-governmental organization. Reality check here, if we were doing this project on government funds I would have to go through a long procurement process of advertising the job, defining all the duties, ensuring all the equal opportunity regulations were satisfied and then possibly getting a low bid by some "average "photographer" who was out of work and willing to take a government job. It made me ill just thinking about it. The "system" really was geared to slow programs down and it hindered you from getting the best people. But there I was-- FREE from all that. We could just pick the best person. How simple and how good it was going to feel.

It didn't take long. One of our local photographer contacts had a friend who had been a freelance film maker for many years. He gave this candidate our phone number and a character by the name of Jeff Hogan gave us a call. Jeff said he was interested in filming for us and that he had a number of good films under his belt. Some were commissioned by National Geographic. He was a one -man operation and assured us he could produce a film for less money than a bigger operation with numerous employees to pay.

I lined up an interview with the board and Jeff arrived right on time with his bran new wife, Karen. The Board of Directors was conducting the interview. The collective experience of the members was impressive – if I do say so myself. Jon Bunderson, attorney who had experience with every con artist in Box Elder County and beyond; Bob Valentine, worked with scads of agencies and businesses; Lee

Shirley, career educator and administrator with Weber County school district; John Cavitt, professor at Weber State University and me. Jeff presented himself so honestly and sincere, we were unanimous from the start. But his new wife Karen was such a sweetheart and "good fit" that she put the interview over the top. Jeff was given the job and it was that quick. I loved doing business that way. Our resident attorney Jon Bunderson said we could do business with Jeff even if we didn't have a contract. Which, by the way, we never took the time to write one up. Better yet, we never wound up needing it either. In Jeff, we got everything he promised and we, of course, held up our end of the bargain. It was an excellent match.

Jeff and I hit it off right away. We were the team who was to get the job done. Of course, I would be relying on the Board of Directors for wisdom and guidance, but the day-to-day filming was up to Jeff and me. To clarify, Jeff was the expert photographer and I was the guide. I knew where to go and Jeff knew how to get the photos. We had a great time together.

Since Jeff was experienced at film production, he helped us envision the process. We needed a story of what we wanted to tell, it had to be scripted and then we had to edit all the film we were about take into 20 minutes or so. We ended up with over 40 hours of film, so editing turned out to be a big deal.

This turned into a two year project and Jeff helped guide us through all the pitfalls. One big piece of advice was not to go through a commercial editing company. He said they are a money sump and he had a friend in Jackson, Wyoming with all the hardware to do the job for a fraction of the cost. That turned out to be a huge money saver. Also, Jeff knew a young musician who would set the film to music at a reasonable cost. He also knew someone to do graphics. Jeff was all about getting the job done without paying an arm and a leg.

I had two main jobs. Guiding Jeff to the right spots at the right time and writing the script. Scrip writing was not my area of expertise and doing it for a yet-to-be completed film made it more difficult. First, I had to write a script and then edit it numerous times. When the script seemed "good," I would try to match it up by sufficiently filming the topic. Simple, but the world of wildlife doesn't work that way. We could not get some images for some of the script. In other instances, we got some good footage, but I had no script to go along with it. So it turns out that the script wasn't edited a few times, it was constantly rewritten. If you like writing – yippee, it would be lots of fun for you. I, on the other hand, would rather do something else since I am hyper most of the time.

As we progressed through the filming and writing, I leaned on Jon Bunderson for help. Jon spent hours going through the script and making improvements. Also, director John Cavitt had a connection at Weber State University in the English Department (Hal Krimmal). Hal also spent time with the script to improve it. In fact, Hal penned the final statement we used to conclude the film (along with some other portions).

At various times, I would ask Jeff to put together some film we could show the other board of directors, just to keep them up to date – and show them the marvelous images he was getting. The mutually beneficial relationship between Jeff and the Friends remained rock solid. Jeff would film and every so often we would ask him to give us a bill. We knew he could use the money because Karen was pregnant by this time as well. They had only been married a few months and I asked Jeff if he was starting a family on the fast track. Jeff said he had no time to lose because he was already 49 (was he ever right). When Jeff submitted a bill he would ask if it was "alright." I would take one look and ask if he was coming out ok, maybe he needed to add more to the bill. Jeff would say he was happy and I told Jeff we were "tickled pink" as well. Bunderson was treasurer as well as president of the Friends, so he would write out a check for Jeff the same day. Jeff said he never got paid that quickly. When working for bigger companies, they were at least 30 days out with their payments. We appreciated Jeff's work and he appreciated getting paid instantly.

Jeff put together a "trailer" about half way through the filming. It included some great wildlife footage as well as some of the script and some music. It was put together quickly to give a basic feel about the film. When we showed it to the full board of directors; they liked the photography and the certain "feel" it conveyed. That is when Bob Valentine came up with another idea. We were hoping to get a well-recognized name to narrate the script. So far, we had talked with Steve Denkers who had a contact with Robert Redford. It sounded promising, but no commitment had yet been made. We wanted a "top drawer" person. Jeff had some contacts, yet still nobody with a solid yes.

Bob said he knew the Director of the Utah Department of Tourism, her name was Leigh Von Der Esch. Bob had a work history with members of her family back in his days with Thiokol. Bob said he would call her and she could view the film and maybe help us with a narrator. Leigh came out shortly thereafter and we took some seats in the Education Center auditorium to review the few minutes of film we had. When the film ended, she was excited and immediately said she could help. She said that Peter Coyote was a possibility because of a good association she had developed with him on a recent film project in Southern Utah. She agreed to give him a call and see what he would say. Needless to say, Peter was agreeable and for a minimal price to become our narrator. Instantly we had improved the status of our film to a new level.

As Karen was nearing the time to deliver their baby, Jeff made a trip to the Refuge specifically to film the large numbers of tundra swans. I lined up an area on the Bear River Club dike dividing the

Refuge and Club. It was "swan central" and I knew Jeff would get some great shots. After a couple of days, I was nearly frozen solid and told Jeff that I was going to Denver to celebrate Christmas. Jeff, a native of Maine, was doing just fine. He decided to stay around for more filming. Jeff's filming was interrupted by a phone call from Karen: she was in labor and had called her midwife. The plan was for Karen to travel to Idaho for the birth. However, there wasn't time for that. Jeff took off for Jackson, picked up Karen and headed to Idaho. The midwife took off and headed west to meet in the middle. Little baby Finn was born in a motel in Idaho Falls shortly after they checked in!

We continued filming and writing. I kept in contact with Leigh on a regular basis. She was familiar with film productions and gave me lots of help to improve our final product. At one session, Leigh told me to think about one sentence to describe the film and stay with it. Man, that was hard but it did help me to focus more. I decided the film was about one of the last of the wildlife Edens in North America.

On another occasion, we were going over the script, one line at a time. That was a GRIND. I personally narrated the script into a section of the film, just to get a feel as to whether it "fit" or not. We were struggling with putting more emotion into the film, so it had more character and would be motivating. I had written a section that began with "The Great Creator." Most of the board members felt it was possibly offensive to people who would not want to hear about God in a refuge film, so I took it out of the paper version of the script that Leigh had. As Leigh was watching snippets of the film and going over the associated script, she came to my narrated paragraph and the images that went with it. I had the volume turned down so we could come up with something new as per the Board's preference. Leigh heard my voice and quickly said, "What was that?" "Turn it up and play it over," Leigh said. "That's perfect, Why did you delete it?" she asked. I told her why and she said referring to the "Great Creator" was not offensive. "let's leave it in." I was thrilled because I wanted to give God credit for all His work. I had a quick visit with Bob Valentine about including it and he was supportive, as was the whole board of directors at the next meeting.

As we progressed with filming, writing and editing, Leigh became more involved on a technical level. Her direction and experience were highly valuable to our direction and progress. In addition to lining up Peter Coyote to narrate the film, Leigh helped with editing and even incorporated the talents of Martha Moensch to assist with the script (you can never get enough help with that). Leigh had access to some funds that could be given to tourism related projects. Our film, "Wings of Thunder" fit that category, so she donated enough to the Friends to cover Peter Coyote's fees, with some left over. Have I mentioned that partnerships are wonderful?

After nearly two years of filming with Jeff through the seasons, it was time to begin the process I was dreading – final editing. We had nearly 40 hours of film that had to be cut down to less than 30 minutes. The script would have to be edited again and again to fit whatever was to become our final film. Jeff suggested that we could save thousands of dollars by doing it ourselves. I never would have dreamed of such a thing, but Jeff insisted he knew a friend in Jackson who had all the equipment we needed and would bill us only a minimal amount to do the work. Of course, that meant that Jeff and I would be involved in the whole process. It isn't something you can drop off and pick up later. You have to direct the entire process. When the time came, I traveled to Jackson to spend several days and produce the "final" film.

Jeff had lined up Troy Beauchamp, a young man who was just entering the film editing business. Troy had a town house in Jackson. An upstairs office was jammed with electronics and screens. Troy had converted all of Jeff's film into digital video and cataloged it so we would have some semblance of order when we started. Surrounded with screens, the three of us just started in. This was going to be a multi- day marathon and after the first hour my ADD was already kicking in. We were in close surroundings and progress was really slow. We ordered in lunch and worked through to supper. We ordered in pizza and kept working. When we quit for the night, I was really played out and we didn't have a lot to show for our efforts yet. I came back the next day and we kept at it. Still, the film was not taking on a *personality* or some kind of a unique feel. It was just a series of wild-life motion pictures without a cohesive story.

Slowly, it began to take on the feel of the Refuge through the seasons. But, our time was drawing to an end and I planned to leave for home that evening after dark. I was totally played out and had no more ideas. At this point, I was just going through the motions as Jeff and Troy kept going over film, adding and taking away scenes. When I had only a few minutes left, I pulled away in the corner and began to write some summary statements that I thought were important for the main ideas to be conveyed by the film. One after another, I began to write down one-sentence ideas as they came to mind. "Where the Bear River Meets the Great Salt Lake, Lies a Modern Day Eden," my thoughts began. From there, other statements poured out of my exhausted brain. A chain of statements followed, concluding with the statement "A story unfolds." I ripped the page out of my spiral note-book and handed the sheet to Jeff as I told him and Troy that I was leaving. I was spent, totally exhausted and needed to get outside immediately. Over several days, my ADD had been building up to dangerous levels. I bailed for home after sunset and spent my drive nearly in a trance, just thinking about the whirlwind of ideas we were trying to bring together into a cohesive film.

Troy and Jeff spent more time bringing the story together. When Jeff came back to Utah with the production, it was essentially done and ready to show the Board of Directors and Leigh. Jeff and Troy had taken my notebook of penciled statements and used them to build an introduction. We were ready to finalize the script and get Peter Coyote involved. After numerous rewrites using some of Hal Crimmel's writing, Martha's editing and Leigh's oversight, we were ready for Peter Coyote's touch. I was excited. I secretly wondered if I would get to meet Peter during this process and what it would be like. No such luck! Peter was going to do his magic from inside an editing booth out-of-state. I just couldn't believe it could be done without more preliminary practice than that.

Peter drove to an editing booth and contacted us by phone. He looked over the script to prepare himself and then it was "showtime." We got to listen as he read through the script – one time and it was final. That was it! "Wow, so that is how a professional does it," I thought to myself. No preliminary recordings, no re-recording over bad spots. Just a quick and flawless read that came out perfectly. Thank you, Peter. Now we were on our way to finishing up the film. We had to add music and some graphics, but the story had come together and the film had a feel that spoke to the heart. We were almost done.

Constant refinements were being made to the film by Jeff, Troy and me. We were on the phone almost daily working through details. When it was essentially done, it was time to show it to the Board of Directors--Jon Bunderson, Bob Valentine, John Cavitt and Lee Shirley. From here on out it would just be a lot of fun. They approved the product and we began to get excited about how we were going to go public with it. Now our attention turned to how we were going to advertise, package and produce copies of the film for distribution and sale. There were more issues and details that none of us were familiar with, but then again, that was "normal" for us.

A major concern was how we were going to design a cover image for the DVD and posters. Jeff's wife, Karen, had a background in art and voiced her interest in doing the artwork design. Hey great! We were comfortable with Karen, she had been by Jeff's side throughout the filming and production of the film. We knew she would do a good job (and at a very reasonable price). I loved making deals like this. What a concept it was. You find a skilled person who will deliver a great product on time for a reasonable price, you make a handshake deal and you are "off to the races." Remember, if this were a government deal, we could NEVER hire the wife of someone on contract. That would violate all kinds of rules, even if they were the best for the job. Also, it would have also taken all kinds of time to run this through the contracting process. But here we were with private funds, so we could just go out and make good deals and be on with it. I had so much fun NOT going through government red tape!

In no time Karen was sending us proposals she had for the artwork. We settled on one and she got right to work finalizing it for both the DVD cover and a poster. Now, it was time to decide when, where and how to make "Wings of Thunder" public. At a board meeting, we decided to plan a formal grand opening event at the Education Center theatre. We would have a coat and tie event and invite all of the dignitaries we could think of. It would include entertainment, food and a few speakers to introduce the film. The evening would end with the first ever showing of the film.

The event was the culmination of over two years work by a lot of people. The Friends of Bear River Refuge had single-handedly made this project their goal and used their funds and members to complete it. The finished product was now available for use on a daily basis in the Education Center at no cost to the government. In addition, DVD's were for sale in the Refuge bookstore. Truly a win-win for everyone involved.

My career had ended two years prior, I had become a full fledged "Friend and volunteer" myself. I was in that slow, and unavoidable, process of drifting away from being an in-touch agency person to an agency ignorant civilian. I got shocked into that fact one day short-ly afterward when a staff person, who will remain anonymous, ap-proached me and blurted out that the Regional Office said the film was out of compliance with the requirement that it be closed captioned for the hearing impaired. He implied that the Friends needed to get that done right away. That is, right away at our own expense.

That hit me all wrong. My first thought was "how ungrateful." The Friends had saved the government loads of time and money al-ready and instead of getting a slap on the back, we got an evaluation that the film needed more work. My instant retort was, "Then tell the Regional Office to come up with the money to do it." I was offended and I let it show. I was also disappointed that someone from the staff could be so unaware of the role the Friends of the Refuge had played in the bigger picture of the restoration as to even bring it up like that. I started to realize that newer staff just did not have the history with the Friends and lacked appreciation for their accomplishments on behalf of the Refuge.

That planted the thought for this book as a necessity to document the history of the Friends of Bear River Refuge as an organization and all volunteers. Their work led the way, and it was being forgotten already, right before my eyes.

After being distributed, "Wings of Thunder" received good re-views. That was good enough for us. Jeff and I remain friends. Sometimes I daydream about spending a day with Jeff back out on the marsh filming wildlife and enjoying his company.

CHAPTER 31

THE ACCESS ROAD, FINALLY

When the Salt Lake began receding in the late 1980's, the access road from Brigham City to the Refuge peeked up to daylight in horrid condition. It had been built in the 1930's and paved through the years that followed. It was minimal, but nevertheless, paved and able to withstand the annual high flows of the Bear River that covered it temporarily most springs. Now, the broken pavement had to be graded out and pushed alongside the right-of-way, so the gravel base could be graded for vehicle travel. It was graded alright, but the result was a deeply-wash boarded surface that was hard on vehicles – and passengers as well. For a while, people were just glad access of any kind was restored. But soon, "everyone" was complaining about how rough the road was and it discouraged lots of would-be visitors, especially those driving cars not suited for rough conditions.

Even though the federal government had built the road originally, Box Elder County now owned it. They were responsible for its maintenance since it was in their inventory of roads. I found myself asking them to grade the road because it was in constant disrepair. My main contact was "Johnny," road Department Supervisor. He oversaw the daily work schedule of all the county employees who worked on the roads of Box Elder County. He could make me happy by just putting the Refuge access road top priority! Right, fat chance. Johnny answered to the Box Elder County Commission, and they wanted to make the voters across the huge county happy. That meant spending most of the time grading farm-to-market transportation corridors. They serviced the Refuge road "when they could." So, I reminded them how bad it was on a constant basis, and they gave it a quick grading once in a great while. I tried pleading with the County Commission from time to time, like when I delivered their "payment in leu of taxes" check. It was a healthy check they looked forward to and it was supposed to be spent on roads and schools. The Refuge sent no kids to school, so you would think that would leave a lot of money to grade our access road with funds left over. That's not how it worked. Jon Buderson knew the commission well since he was County Attorney. He did what he could from time to time.

Over the early 1990's, the access road became a sore subject with Refuge visitors – including hunters. When I contacted visitors, I could expect to hear "When are YOU going to fix the road?" I repeated for the *millionth* time, "Go talk to the County Commission, it belongs to them." That didn't help, of course, but it gave me something to say. The county, in turn, would tell me that the federal government should pave the road because it goes to the bird refuge. They held to their schedule of grading the access road occasionally. That was that.

The solution was obvious, we needed to quit pointing the finger at each other and go after funding somehow to just get the road paved. I had no pot of money to go after with the Fish and Wildlife Service, so it just looked like the road would remain rough gravel indefinitely. By this time, Bob Valentine was Director of the Box Elder County Department of Economic Development. He acted to complete the first step for an access road.

Since Brigham City was only accessible from I-15 off the 1100 South Ramp and the Corinne interchange, it was an economic issue to have an additional interchange on the Forest Street intersection. Bob went right to work on that: he tapped into state highway funds to get the interchange built. That sounds easy after the fact, but it took hours of behind-the-scenes work to gain the support of the myriad of officials and committees that approve projects of that size. Bob was a master at that kind of work. He would address each hurdle through a long process like that until it was done. It also helped that he had the support of Representative Jim Hansen and our two Senators-Hatch and Bennett.

With the Forest Street interchange completed, Bob went to work on the Federal Highway Commission. They are loaded with money, but just try to get some. It takes some political influence along with paperwork that just doesn't quit. The first breakthrough came prior to the 2002 Olympics when the State of Utah was concerned with having good access to Olympic venues. I received the wonderful news that we were getting enough funding to begin the planning process – which is no small thing. I was certain that once we started getting funds, more would come until the road was done.

Then I was educated in the way that Utah Department of Transportation (UDOT) handled Federal appropriations. Silly me. I thought that money "earmarked" for the Refuge road had to go to that project even though the money was filtered through UDOT. By that I mean, the federal government handed UDOT the money specified for the Refuge. UDOT was the "middle man." As I was waiting for UDOT to relinquish the funds, they called a meeting and told me that the funds earmarked for the Refuge were going to be used to complete the road to Soldier Hollow for the Olympics. "What? You just take the money for the Refuge road and use it however you want?" I asked. Their Director informed me that they had authority to redirect all the funds they receive, and I had no recourse. I was dumfounded. It was just blatant highway robbery as far as I was concerned. But, "watcha gonna do?"

Predictably, I went right to Bob Valentine. He let it be known to the state highway Director that he was highly offended by her behavior, but her decision to steal our money stuck. Bob let it slide and went right to work for more money in the next fiscal year. And what do you know, he was successful again with another "earmarked" appropriation for the access road. And guess what, UDOT announced they were going to take that money and redirect it for one of their priorities. Enough was enough, Bob contacted Senator Bennett and told him what was going on and we needed our money. I got a call from Bob telling me to call UDOT and have them attend a meeting with Senator Bennett's staff. I really felt a little "cocky" whenever Bob was about to get things straight for the Refuge. I was powerless, yet Bob was making things happen on my behalf.

UDOT knew what was up and the Director's staff arrived at my office right on time. We gathered around the conference table-Bob, the Senator's staff, UDOT officials and me. I was itching to see how UDOT was going to get "taken to the woodshed." Before I could utter a word, a UDOT staffer stood up and announced that all our money had been restored into the Refuge account. I was happy, but inside my prideful self was a little disappointed because they avoided getting beat up and I wanted to see them squirm. Oh well, the objective was met and that was the main thing. I just needed to get my pride in check.

Originally I was hoping for a meeting that would beat up on UDOT, but it turned into a productive discussion on how the road plans would be scheduled right away that fiscal year. Great, we were on our way even though it would take years before construction would begin. Road building these days is a process shackled with a complexity of committees, executive approvals and all sorts of red tape. It seems like *everybody* gnaws away at your budget. To make matters worse, as the funds are bled off, the process slows down. When more money is needed, it is all up to you to get more appropriated. It really is quite frustrating.

The Federal Highway Administration took the lead as soon as the funding started. A long, laborious process of road design started. Silly me, I thought that since a road had already been built and been in operation since the 1930's, a rebuild would be a quick and easy engineering task. You know, just go back over the road foot by foot using some modern engineering and you will have a new plan in short order. Oh, no, no, no. It doesn't work like that at all. The process requires starting over from scratch and using some very expensive remote sensing technology. It begins with some exacting surveys that could split a gnat's eye lash. Now I have no problem with good surveys, but this required a team of engineers and months of analysis. When the draft was done, we had to compare it with actual features on the ground to prove its accuracy. I was ready to be impressed with advanced surveying and engineering. Instead, we found areas where culverts were needed, but not planned and vise -versa. We also told the engineers that the roadway would have to include segments where the grade was lower to let annual floodwaters of the River flow over. That suggestion was rejected immediately. "We don't plan Texas Crossings anymore because they are too dangerous," the engineering department replied. As we neared the end of the first phase of planning, the engineers totaled up how many feet of bridges would be necessary to pass the required volume of water and it cranked the price tag on the road to an astronomical number. They eventually decided that Texas Crossings were feasible in our case. Keep in mind the original road had the same design, so we were not doing anything drastic.

As the project wound its way through the army of engineers at the Federal Highway Administration, specialized experts in their fields of expertise were assigned specific tasks. There was no single engineer who stayed with the planning from start to finish. Usually, the newbie engineer would look at the project from his office in Denver and say something skeptical after looking at the raw data (soils, gradient, river flows, etc.). Then I would explain that there was a road already built on the right-of-way that had lasted from the 1930's until the great flood with no problem. "We are just replacing an existing road," I would explain. And so, it went, engineer after engineer. I marveled at how the original road was designed by Vanez Wilson (the first refuge manager) using survey equipment that is much less accurate than today's laser instruments, yet Vanez got it right. I concluded that there is no substitute for being familiar with the environment you are working in. Vanez knew the landscape in all its seasons and extremes because all his survey work was on foot. He must have developed a "feel", or call it judgment, about how to build things across the mudflats. No textbook information can replace the on-the-ground experience gained from years on site. When I looked at the costs of numerous "offsite" engineers and their required information (laser overflights, etc.), we could have easily hired a full time engineer on staff for a number of years and been way better off financially. Unfortunately, the government does not work that way. We simply had to work through the established process, as inefficient as it was. And, to say nothing about how that disturbed me...

I retired in the middle of the process. My deputy, Steve Hicks, carried on with overseeing the planning. Eventually, the plans were completed and the project was placed out for bids. It turned out to be an excellent road, even though the cost was higher than I could have ever imagined. I attended a special event held by the Refuge to commemorate opening the road to the public. I had been retired for a while and it was good to see the road was FINALLY completed. It seemed surreal to be sitting in the audience as a spectator, listening to various speakers. I looked around for Bob Valentine and Jon Bunderson, but neither one were there. I felt all alone and somewhat "blank" that they were not part of the celebration. It was a dream we had all shared and it is something we can be proud of.

When you drive the road today, it is smooth and wide. A bike lane is marked out on one side, encouraging people to exercise while enjoying nature. That feature alone brings me joy, even though I suffered from sticker shock initially.

SUMMARY AND CONCLUSION

Between 1910 and 1928, a generation rose up and accomplished a conservation marvel. When scant few examples were out there to follow, they wrote history themselves by establishing Bear River Migratory Bird Refuge. Six decades later, another generation made history once again by meeting the challenge of restoring the flood demolished Refuge. The torch will soon be passed on yet again, this time to a new and much different generation. The question is, will they sustain the conservation ethic? Will our dwindling wildlands and wildlife have the same draw to the next generation? Or will the lure of electronic recreation dull their interest in the natural world? The fate of the Refuge is in the balance. Protecting and sustaining the Refuge will require a sacrifice of other priorities, especially in our modern world that offers all kinds of exciting entertainment.

In 1910 the first challenge went out loud and clear, but it was not voiced in a well delivered speech. Rather, it was from the silent suffering and death of waterfowl which numbered in the millions. As their rotting carcasses filled the landscape, local people took up the challenge to heal a broken landscape and bring back the once abundant flocks. We have only scant records of the details. We don't even know the names of those locals who championed the cause by organizing the Congressional effort and the concurrent support of Utah's government. However, we do know of their success and the end product; it was no less than the establishment of Bear River Migratory Bird Refuge in April of 1928. We also know that 3 million dollars was appropriated, a huge sum in those years, with the expectation that the area would be developed into a show case of wildlife conservation. And that it was—until the flood destruction of the 1980's.

In 1989 the challenge went out again in much the same manner. It was a silent call for help by the same voiceless marsh that had been stripped bare by the briny floodwaters of Great Salt Lake. It was a time that tested the level of dedication held by volunteers of the Brigham City area.

Answering the challenge was a corps of local residents who would become champions for the cause of Refuge restoration and join hand in hand with a small, but dedicated, Refuge staff. Adding to the ranks of the local volunteer army were businesses, politicians, philanthropists, organizations, Brigham City, Box Elder County and so many others. Together, they not only restored the "old" Refuge, but rebuilt it even better than before. After the Refuge's wildlife habitat was restored, their attention turned to completing an Education Center and replacing the paved access road. They rebirthed the Refuge to face a new century with challenges from an ever increasing human population. Because of their accomplishments and success they are an uncommon generation.

There is an energy, a mysterious grip that the Bear River marshes exert over those who spend time in her embrace. It is one of the few remaining places where marshlands dominate the landscape. You can be enveloped by the horizon-to-horizon scenery filled with a myriad of living things. The marshes and the fragile balance of life they sustain somehow transport visitors to a more basic and less complicated lifestyle. If only for a brief time, one can leave the baggage of a complicated 21st century life to find in the Bear River marshes a closer connection with family, friends and the Great Creator. The Refuge environment is not always comfortable for visitors seeking an experience with wildlands and wildlife; cold or heat along with violent storms can test the stamina of a bird watcher, photographer or hunter. But meeting the challenge of whatever the environment dishes out is part of what makes a lifetime memory. Many a young hunter has been tested physically with a dawn to dark excursion in icy water. Memories of a day with family in an uninterrupted immersion in marsh, sky and birds can shape the values and character of a son or daughter. Whether it is sighting that special bird to check off on a life list or bagging a drake in full plumage as he is drawn into a spread of decoys, the sense of wonder in the wilds of the marsh will etch itself forever in a special corner of the mind.

The intricate weaving of water, earth and sky with a myriad of wild creatures brings a calming peace. It is the ultimate created reality of all things living within an interconnected web of life. Our desires to be refreshed are fulfilled by a chorus of bird calls and endless landscape flooding our senses from all directions.

To volunteers, employees and visitors alike, I hope you experience the mystique of Bear River Refuge for yourself and develop a personal relationship with *her*. May she forever give her special blessings to all visitors coming from all around the world and retain her christened title in 1928, "The World's Greatest Gamebird Refuge." And most of all, may she retain that delicate harmony among vibrant wildlife communities that the Great Creator placed in this unique area.

As for the legacy, it is a gentle voice that speaks to the heart and soul of all visitors who venture within her boundaries. The mystique of wilderness, the Creator's plants and animals in perfect harmony, quietly fills an inner void left by civilization. It gives a calming salve, a solace, a refreshment and inspiration to those who seek respite in her gentle embrace.

May the time and effort the community of volunteers gave for the restoration of Bear River Migratory Bird Refuge be long remembered. It was their sacrifice and labor of love that brought forth this wonder from the brink of ruin.

EPILOGUE

Bear River Migratory Bird Refuge has been in good hands since 1928. Those hands, from the local grassroots, are what birthed one of the nation's greatest wildlife refuges. Those same hands promoted its virtues over the decades, and with devotion they re-birthed it during the years of restoration 1989- 2008.

I have recorded some of the champions of that restoration, but I have been unable to mention many more who were involved. I am profoundly sorry to all those who were not mentioned by name and yet still led an active part.

Soon after the restoration, the nation's priorities shifted away from conservation. Year after year, budgets were reduced for land management agencies within the Department of Interior-- especially so for the U.S. Fish and Wildlife Service. The relentless budget declines forced a reduction in staff and conservation work. My occasional visits to the Refuge administrative offices over the years seemed more like a visit to a morgue. Cuts in the Refuge staff were crippling to wildlife management and public services. The remaining personnel were just trying to hold on by doing critical work to keep the Refuge in operation at a minimal level. It requires a basic core of employees to administer, oversee and manage 110 square miles of land and 1.2 million acre/feet of water. As staff reductions continued over the years, even basic management activities could not all get accomplished. Hard choices had to be made as to what would be done and what would be let go.

It is my hope and dream that national priorities will once again re-align with protecting and managing our natural resources so that important conservation work will be accomplished and places like Bear River Migratory Bird Refuge will meet their potential.

I hope this brief history of volunteers and Friends will inspire others to join their ranks. The work can be demanding, both in time and effort, but it is worth the personal investment. Whether you help restore wildlife habitat, maintain facilities, interpret some aspect of nature or help connect people with the magic of Bear River Refuge; your personal investment will reward you. It has for many volunteers so far, and it has for me as I now serve as a volunteer on occasion.

As for me, the author of this manuscript, I can only hope I get a cushy deal on some campus where I get paid loads of money to do absolutely nothing except talk about the bygone days of my work with the Friends Of Bear River Refuge organization and the many volunteers. So, I will just wait for the first offer.

I'm still waiting….. And waiting…..

DONORS FOR THE EDUCATION CENTER BUILDING FUND

GOAL: $1.5 MILLION

ORGANIZATIONS:

- The Bear River Club
- Box Elder County
- Brigham City
- Browning
- Emma Eccles Jones Foundation
- George S. Eccles Foundation
- Chris Ford Foundation
- Jones Family Foundation
- Royal Barney Foundation
- Jessie Quinney Foundation
- S.G. and S.E. Denkers Family Foundation
- Utah Wetlands
- Wal;-Mart

- Willard Eccles Foundation
- L.T. and J.T. Foundation
- National Fish and Wildlife Foundation
- Melanie Spriggs Foundation
- Peterson Mason Foundation
- Ralph Nye Foundation
- Raymond T. Duncan

INDIVIDUALS:

- Elizabeth and Stephen Bechtel Jr.
- Riley Bechtel
- Steve Bechtel
- Frosty Braden
- Joris W. Brinkerhoff
- Zach Brinkerhoff, Jr.
- Stephen Denkers
- Dorothy Egan
- Florence Gilmore
- Dick Heckert
- John F. Hotchkis
- John Kadlec
- William C. Morris
- Wayne Martenson
- John and Marlene Peters
- Gary Slot

Since 1929, Brigham City has maintained an arch over main street declaring it as the "Gateway to the World's Greatest Gamebird Refuge."

Receding floodwaters in the late 1980's exposed the extent of damage. This southerly view of the mouth of the Bear River shows the headquarters ruins and barren landscape.

A close-up of the ruins at the headquarters site. An office, Visitor Center, shop and residences were destroyed. Note the bridge decks across the mouth of the river; they are knocked off their supporting foundation walls.

Looking west over the Bear River Channel in 1990. The landscape was entirely devoid of vegetation.

Remains of the shop as floodwaters receded.

Typical road and dike damage from the flood. The surface was eroded several feet below the grade.

236

Salt water inundated all impoundments as seen in this photo of Unit 5. All vegetation important to migratory birds was killed by the high salt concentrations in the water. Bird use was almost nil.

Even towers, used by refuge visitors for decades, were toppled by floodwaters and ice flows.

As flood waters slowly rose during the mid-1980's, the entire headquarters area--including a newly dedicated Visitor Center— was destroyed.

Throughout the 1990's, access to the refuge was sketchy in the spring when peak flows arrived in the Bear River from melting snow packs in the mountains.

Typical condition of small water control structures before restoration.

Congressman James V. Hansen (left) with Ducks Unlimited personnel announce a $5,000 grant to the volunteers. This donation was among the first funding received and was used to purchase basic supplies to repair water control structures and rehabilitate dikes.

A Brigham City lumber yard donated planks to the volunteers for fabricating flashboards.

Bob Ebeling and Bob Balmer building flashboards in a shop donated by the Lilypond Corporation. These flashboards were installed to enable refilling Refuge marshes with fresh water from the Bear River.

239

Operating a dozer transferred from the Golden Spike National Historic Site, volunteers cleared debris from the old headquarters site.

A portion of new pipeline installed from the Bear River channel to Unit 2B. The project was completely funded by private donations.

As part of reopening the 12 mile auto tour route on July 4, 1990, the volunteers replaced previously used interpretive panels that had been removed ahead of the flood.

Reassembling the historic boundary sign that was demolished by floodwaters and ice flows. The individual planks were recovered from the mud after water receded. After being repainted and reassembled, the sign was erected for the July 4, 1990, opening of the Auto Tour Route.

Whitaker Construction donated a grader with operator to smooth dike surfaces enough to allow vehicle access. This was the first dike repair after the flood.

The author (left) with Bob Ebeling enjoying a few moments together on the refuge in 1990 in the early days of the restoration.

The author (left) with Bob Ebeling enjoying a few moments together on the refuge in 1990 in the early days of the restoration.

Bob and Darleen Ebeling (1990). Darleen became a photographer for the volunteers as they began restoration activities. Note the ATV: it was privately owned. At this point in time the refuge did not own any pickups or equipment.

July 4, 1990, ceremony hosted by the Friends of Bear River Refuge to mark the opening of the 12 mile Auto Tour Route. All work and funding was organized and completed by volunteers.

Volunteers working with Utah Airboat Association members built and distributed floating nest structures for ducks and geese. All materials and services were donated.

Norm Layton (right) teams up with Bob Balmer to activate another water control structure.

Unit 5 contains a 12 bay water control structure. Each bay required up to 10 flashboards, which translates into a lot of back breaking work. The yellow pickup, one of the many privately owned vehicles used during the restoration, belonged to Bob Ebeling.

Over 30 concrete water control structures had to be renovated before they could begin to impound fresh water in 1990. Using donated lumber, volunteers installed temporary catwalks and replaced flashboards. Note the yellow dodge pickup, termed Old Yeller. It was donated to us by another refuge.

Bob Ebeling (left) and Jesse Roberts placing flashboards into a structure.

As though the volunteers did not have enough to do already, a botulism epidemic killed thousands of waterfowl in the summer of 1990. Using their own boats, volunteers scoured the marshes for carcasses to remove. Jesse Roberts is preparing to dump one day's pick-up of waterfowl into a burial pit.

Although devoid of vegetation at first, the impoundments soon had algae which was followed by more desirable marsh vegetation.

Ryan Trout, the author's son, joined the corps of volunteers during the summer of 1990. He was given the radio identification code "00" and provided the services of a young strong back according to Bob Ebeling.

The author (right front) enjoying a short break with the volunteers as they planted alkali bulrush in Unit 3. The volunteers enjoyed each other as much as the work they accomplished. Back row, left to right: Vicki Hirschboeck, Rich Iwanski, Lee Weeks, Norm Layton, Mark Laneer and Jesse Roberts. Front row: Quinn Eskelsen, Jerry Keller, Bob Ebeling and Al Trout.

With use of an airboat, alkali bulrush seed was planted in Units 2 and 3 to speed up marsh recovery. L to R, Lee Weeks, Quinn Eskelsen, Norm Layton, Brandon Serna, Darleen Ebeling, unknown, and Bob Ebeling.

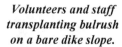

Volunteers and staff transplanting bulrush on a bare dike slope.

Tom Walker (center), helps to place the strapping for the crane to lift the decks.

With the first deck in place, the crane moved out to repeat the same process for each successive deck.

The bridge slowly took shape.

The completed job, ready for travel and work to begin on the dikes around Unit 2. Radial gates, to control waterflows, will eventually be replaced on this structure to reactivate the water management system.

Tying off rebar before placing concrete on the spillway of the Jamison Unit. The volunteers designed, funded and provided all construction tasks for creating this 600 acre wetland.

The Jamison Unit filled with water soon after the dike and spillway was completed. Volunteers wanted the area to be named after Max Jamison, the person who envisioned and championed the project.

Volunteers taking time out for a photograph after erecting a refuge sign. Left to right are Tom Walker, Quinn Eskelsen, Bob Ebeling, Norm Layton, Bob Balmer and Jesse Roberts.

A moment of humor in the early years of the restoration with small, but close knit staff. (Left to right) the author, Cherry Fisher, Claire Caldes and Kieth Hansen

Volunteer Bob Green poses by a wetland he designed and helped develop. Bob, a retired professional engineer in water rights and water management, spent much of his time alongside our staff providing information and guidance.

A typical section of dike being brought up to grade after the flood lowered the dikes an average of four feet. The entire restoration resulted in rehabilitating 50 miles of historic dikes and building an additional 50 miles of new dikes.

Placing concrete for a new boat ramp to provide marsh access for both hunters and refuge employees.

Rich Iwanski, maintenance supervisor, at work setting grade with surveying equipment.

Maintenance supervisor Rich Iwanski poses next to his personally designed pre-cast structure. His reusable forms saved time and money when a culvert with flashboards was required.

Numerous pre-cast concrete parts were assembled on site to build a large water control structure. This design was developed by Rich Iwanski and precluded the need to build forms on site which saved labor and money.

A nearly completed pre-cast water control structure designed by Rich Iwanski. This design not only saved time but thousands of dollars as well.

Peter Olson (volunteer) works with Rich Iwanski on the inlet to O line canal as they prepare to set the radial gates.

Concrete work was a never ending chore. Rod Jacobson (foreground) works with Rich Iwanski to fill foundation forms on the O line inlet structure.

Although draglines had become obsolete, Butch Robinson Construction used one to accomplish work in selected locations.

By December 1996, many of the Refuge marshes had made full recovery. This dawn scene was looking southwest in Unit 9.

Restored marshes, with the Promontory Mountains for a background, show off their beauty.

One of the many developed wetlands in the Grassland Habitat Unit. This easterly view features a backdrop of the Wasatch Mountains.

Bob Valentine (L) and Larry Shanks were the two instrumental people in acquiring appropriations for the Education Center.

Bob Valentine gave untold hours of effort to the restoration. Beyond his refuge work, Bob was a close personal friend.

Bob Valentine (L) requesting support for special funding from J.J. Brown, Senator Bennett's chief of staff. Every annual visit was successful in securing funds.

Congressman James V. Hansen and Bob Valentine discussing Refuge funding needs for the restoration. Refuge expansion, improvement of the water management system and the Education Center was made possible by their efforts.

Funding for the Education Center was garnered over a number of years by annual visits to Washington D.C. to meet with Senators, Congressmen, agencies and non-governmental organizations. (L to R) Bob Valentine, Larry Shanks, the author and Congressman Jim Hansen pose during a briefing on funding needs.

Bob Valentine (L) discuss Refuge funding needs with Alan Freemyer of Congressman Jim Hansen's staff. Since it is illegal for government employees to ask for money, all funding requests were made by our "Friends of the Refuge" organization.

Friends give $1 million 2004

THERE'S A SECRET to writing a $1 million check - you have to crowd the nine zeroes in order to fit them in the space allowed. Just as of the Bear River Refuge Board of Trustee members Jon Bunderson and Bob Valentine. They presented the donation to Bear River Bird Refuge Director Al Trout (left) last week. "This is the first million of a $1.5 million obligation the Friends have to the refuge," stated. The donation will create the impetus to get things underway to build the visitors center. The project will be put out on bid in future. It is anticipated actual construction will begin by spring.

Photograph published in the Box Elder News and Journal when the Friends of the Refuge donated $1.5 million for construction of the Education Center

Cover image of brochure advertising the custom engraved shotgun donated by Browning Arms Company.

256

CPSIA information can be obtained
at www.ICGtesting.com
Printed in the USA
BVHW011139040322
630681BV00007B/160

9 781685 153274